MOUNTAIN BIKE HANDBOOK

796
.6
Van

Van der Plas, Rob, 1938-
    Mountain bike handbook / Robert van der Plas ;
[translated by Elisabeth R. Reinersmann]. -- New York :
Sterling Pub. Co., c1991.
    128 p. : ill.

Includes index.
06547176   LC:91013643   ISBN:0806984252 (pbk.)

1. All terrain cycling. 2. All terrain bicycles. I. Title

MOUNTAIN BIKE HANDBOOK

Robert van der Plas

 Sterling Publishing Co., Inc.   New York

Translated by Elisabeth R. Reinersmann
English translation edited by Keith L. Schiffman

Library of Congress Cataloging-in-Publication Data
van der Plas, Rob, 1938–
    [Mountain Bike Know-How. English]
    Mountain bike handbook / by Robert van der Plas.
      p. cm.
    Translation of: Mountain Bike Know-How.
    Includes index.
    ISBN 0-8069-8424-4
    1. All terrain cycling. 2. All terrain bicycles. I. Title.
GV1056.V3613   1991
796.6—dc20   91-13643
                                  CIP

10 9 8 7 6 5 4 3 2 1

English translation © 1991 by Sterling Publishing Company
387 Park Avenue South, New York, N.Y. 10016
Original edition published in Germany under the title
Mountain Bike Know-How
© 1990 by BLV Verlagsgesellschaft mbH, Munich
Distributed in Canada by Sterling Publishing
c/o Canadian Manda Group, P.O. Box 920, Station U
Toronto, Ontario, Canada M8Z 5P9
Distributed in Great Britain and Europe by Cassell PLC
Villiers House, 41/47 Strand, London WC2N 5JE, England
Distributed in Australia by Capricorn Ltd.
P.O. Box 665, Lane Cove, NSW 2066
Printed and bound in Hong Kong

Sterling ISBN 0-8069-8424-4 Trade

Contents

1
A New Era in Bicycling

The mountain bike symbolizes the phenomenal bicycle boom

Since the mid 1980s a true bicycling revolution has taken place. At first labelled a passing "fad," and looked upon with amusement, a totally new type of bicycle was born. The wide-tired mountain bike conquered bicyclists' hearts, even those who had never been comfortable with the ten-speed. After it had taken America by storm, it spread all over Europe. Among adults, the mountain bike outsells all others.

Mountain bikes are not only bought, they're also used. Unlike those who bought the ten-speed, people who buy a mountain bike do use it—off-road or on the road. It is as useful for daily commuting as it is for sports and recreation.

This new versatile bike is built to handle any terrain, and is designed so that anyone can handle it with ease—regardless of age, gender, or experience. It is as easy to handle for the well-coordinated as it is for those who are "all thumbs." Straight handlebars guarantee a good overall view of traffic, as well as easy access to brake levers that respond exceptionally well. The gearshift levers—easy to reach and easy to use—make hill climbing and riding downhill a cinch, because of the location of the center of gravity and a powerful, reliable brake system.

Despite all these advantages, most mountain bikers still miss half the fun. They ride their bikes correctly, but they don't make use of the bike's special qualities. Let's see how to get more out of riding your bike. The mountain bike—equipped with the right accessories—lets you do things you never thought possible. Properly adjusted, expertly maintained, and skillfully ridden, you'll get a great deal of fun out of your mountain bike. Armed with the information in this book, you'll ride safer, faster, and further.

The Mountain Bike and Its Offspring

The original mountain bike, developed in California in the early 1980s, was primarily a "fun bike," designed for off-road downhill racing followed by a long, uphill struggle in low gear. Knobby high-pressure tires were supposed to give sufficient traction and smooth out rough terrain. Powerful brakes and wide, flat handlebars allowed drivers to maintain control over the bike even under extreme situations. Only later, when mountain bikes became available commercially (this happened rather quickly in the USA) would the bike be used for more practical purposes. It did not take long for people to realize that this uncomplicated machine was an ideal vehicle for touring (able to carry the necessary luggage), as well as for everyday city use.

The mountain bike made its way to Europe, where two mountain bike derivatives were developed. These two bikes later found followers worldwide: the city bike, and what I like to call the touring mountain bike.

The city bike, with thick tires and all the necessary accessories, was designed for daily use in traffic, for shopping as well as for commuting to work.

The touring mountain bike has everything necessary for an extensive tour. Solidly built, like the regular mountain bike, this model has sturdy

luggage racks, water-bottle cages, a sturdy guard for the derailleur (should the bike fall on its side), fenders, and a kickstand.

Yet another version of the mountain bike is the hybrid. The tires of this version are narrower and the tire tread is not quite as deep as that of the mountain bike. While this bike is suitable for off-road use, it is not sufficient for really rough terrain. It was meant primarily for use on mixed road surfaces. It has only the barest accessories and is, therefore, more closely related to the mountain bike than to the city bike. It is also much easier to propel than the latter.

Interestingly enough, a whole new sport has sprung up: mountain bike racing. In some respects this sport is very different from conventional cyclo-cross. For instance, during a mountain bike race, the racer will ride the same bike from start to finish, while in a cyclo-cross race the riders are free to switch bikes as they see fit and often carry their bikes nearly as long as they ride them. The rules of the sport also vary a great deal. For some events,

the race is decided on the best downhill time; in other events, power and stamina or sheer agility are deciding factors. Although America is the pioneer in this field, this sport has seen much activity in Europe. The Grundig Cup Championship is an internationally recognized series of races. It is also rather easy for a group of mountain bikers to get together to hold their very own competition, in addition to sanctioned races.

Consideration for the Environment

Before we list all the positive aspects of mountain biking, let's take a look at the negative aspects. Because this vehicle can get you just about anywhere, it also gets you where you're *not* welcome. On some narrow trails and off-road, the mountain bike can do damage. Soil erosion can be caused or aggravated by braking, steering, or accelerating on soft soil. The resulting damage to the surface can interfere with water drainage, and it can harm plant roots.

Fauna and flora must be respected. You should only use existing trails, and even here you must be careful not to frighten wildlife. In some instances you may have to avoid a particular area altogether. The biker is much faster, and often even quieter than a hiker or a horseback rider. The sudden appearance of a mountain bike might cause fear and panic among animals already used to hikers or horseback riders.

Then there are our fellow travellers: hikers, horseback riders, as well as farmers and forest rangers. We have to share nature with all of them. Therefore, be courteous. They are not only to be endured, but to be accepted—see yourself as one of them, feeling true kinship with nature and the environment. Be considerate towards other trail users. Only then will we be able to enjoy nature—each in his own way.

In the last few years, attempts have been made to prohibit (or at least to severely restrict) the use of mountain . bikes. On Mt. Tamalpais (California), many trails are closed to bikers, and

strict speed limits are enforced on others. This phenomenon is spreading. In some Swiss tourist areas, the use of bicycles anywhere outside city limits has been prohibited outright, and a few German tourist towns have considered similar measures. From an ecological point of view, these drastic measures are really not justified; the restrictions pertain to roads that are already much frequented (summer and winter). The effect of the amount of mountain bike traffic would be minimal compared to the use these trails now get.

In Marin County (California), the birthplace of the mountain bike, authorities, prompted by members of various horseback riding clubs,

nature and tourist groups, do not hesitate to confront reckless mountain bikers. A speed limit of 15 mph was instituted. It's strictly enforced with the aid of radar traps, resulting in fines of $200.00 or more.

There is very little that bikers can do. If you are in places frequented by hikers and horseback riders, remember that they enjoyed their sports there long before mountain bikes arrived, and they have the right to enjoy their leisure time undisturbed and in safety. Leave your bike at home once in a while and go on a hike. You might learn about some of those "reckless" mountain bikers and notice how irritating "they" can be. If bikers stay away from the places where

they're not wanted, they'll have a chance to claim *their* right to alternative trails.

Of course, mountain bikes are not being used only in sensitive natural environments. In fact, several studies have shown that the majority of mountain bikers use their bikes primarily on regular, paved streets and roads.

Even there it is important to be considerate. Other road users have a right to expect predictable and considerate behavior from you. On a mountain bike, it is sometimes possible to react to a particular traffic situation with very quick moves that other people do not necessarily expect. Even riding on a normal street, think what the consequences of your action might have on others.

About This Book

This book is meant to help the reader to use his mountain bike as effectively as possible, and to help the reader get as much joy as possible from his wonderful bike. The mountain bike is as fantastic for women as it is for men. Because of the more upright seating position, the lower frame construction and the excellent gearing, the mountain bike is particularly well-suited to women. When we use "he" in the text, we do so only to avoid the rather cumbersome use of he/she or (s/he).

This book is meant to aid not only those who already own a mountain bike, but also those who are searching for one. Chapters 2 and 3 are particularly helpful when shopping for the best possible bike. Reading those two chapters will also be very informative to those who already own a bike, because they will then be able to better understand, and thereby to make better use of

their bikes. Chapter 4 discusses accessories and clothing. After covering the bike and the necessary accessories, the next chapters describe how to have the best and most comfortable ride. These chapters discuss gearing, steering, braking, as well as proper maneuvering of the bike. Chapters 7 and 8 deal with handling the bike off-road, away from paved roads. These two chapters also discuss bike control and orientation in the outback.

Chapter 9 covers health aspects of mountain biking. Here you'll find very specific suggestions for fitness training. This chapter also covers the dangers that are a common part of riding a mountain bike—how to avoid them, and how to deal with injuries, if they should occur.

Chapter 10 discusses the maintenance and care of your mountain bike. The reader won't be burdened with too much technical information, but the most important aspects of the subject are covered. You will find here concise information for a regular maintenance schedule and basic repairs. Particular attention

is paid to tires, gearing, and brakes.

At the conclusion of the book, you'll find development and gear tables, a frame-size chart, a troubleshooting guide, and a metric-equivalents chart.

2
The Mountain Bike

**The quintessence of more than one hundred years
of bicycle development
Ideas for customizing a mountain bike**

This chapter introduces you to the particulars of a mountain bike. This bike differs greatly in appearance from other bicycles, but more than just looks make this bike different. More than appearance alone gave the mountain bike, with its particular qualities, its reputation. If you do not yet own a mountain bike, read this chapter; it will make you a better consumer when you are ready to buy one. You will find information in subsequent chapters that will help you to buy the right bike and the proper accessories.

Construction of a Mountain Bike

An illustration of a typical mountain bike is shown on pages 14 and 15.
  Let's focus on the characteristics of a mountain bike and what makes this bike different from other bicycles (the ten-speed bike, for example). A true mountain bike differs from other wide-tire bikes in the following ways:

- The mountain bike has 18 or even 21 gears, covering a very wide gear ratio.
- The fat tires are mounted on lightweight aluminum rims; they can be inflated to high air pressure. Most tires have a very deep tread pattern ("profile").
- Special brakes are so strong that it is possible to bring the bike to a complete halt even under the most unfavorable circumstances.
- The steering system and the frame geometry allow the biker to steer the mountain bike accurately and

13

SADDLE

SEAT POST

QUICK-RELEASE
BINDER BOLT

CANTILEVER (OR SPECIAL)
BRAKE

REAR WHEEL

FRONT
DERAIL

FREEWHEEL WITH
SPROCKETS

REAR DERAILLEUR

BOTTOM BRAC

CHAIN

Parts of a

14

HANDLEBARS ———— ○ ———— THUMB SHIFTER

BRAKE LEVER

HANDLEBAR STEM

CANTILEVER BRAKE

FRONT WHEEL

FRONT FORK

CHAIN RINGS

K ARM

PEDAL

ntain bike

safely, no matter if he's going uphill, downhill, on rough trails, or on regular roads.

- A mountain bike has a quick-release seat-post lever that allows the rider to make necessary saddle-height adjustment. For instance, a saddle must be lowered for improved balance when riding downhill.
- A mountain bike and its parts are rigidly constructed to give it stability without adding unnecessary weight.

The mountain bike consists of a main frame to which all its other parts are mounted. The many different parts, shown in the following sketches and photos, can best be described by grouping them together according to their functions, which we have done in the following chapters. The first mountain bikes, made in the late 1970s and early 1980s, were built from parts that had proven to be effective for similar purposes. Moped brake levers from Magura were combined with Mafac cyclo-cross brakes. It didn't take long for the manufacturers of bicycle parts

to realize that the customer and the bike manufacturers needed parts specifically designed for mountain bikes.

The Japanese manufacturer Shimano (in particular) soon began to design a wide range of components that included everything needed for building a mountain bike. The Shimano component group "Deore XT II" is considered tops for the construction of first-class mountain bikes, with brilliantly polished, precisely fitting, and smoothly functioning components. Other companies, who were unable to produce the many different components needed for a bike were forced to cooperate with other manufacturers. That led to the development of many of the existing component groups like the SunTour group, who have brakes made by Dia-Compe, and cranks from Sugino or SR. The European bicycle recently also began to take the mountain bike business seriously. Campagnolo recently offered the nice but heavy Euclid mountain bike component group, followed by the Centaur, a less clumsy version. Also very promising are the products of

Sachs-Huret, a French subsidiary of German Fichtel & Sachs. Their affordable, well-functioning components compete successfully with bikes from the Far East in the same price range.

Components of the Mountain Bike

The diagram on pages 14 and 15 shows a typical mountain bike. The most important parts and accessories are labelled. Let's group them according to function:

- Frame
- Steering system
- Saddle and seat post
- Wheels
- Drivetrain
- Gearing system
- Brakes
- Accessories

The Frame

The diagram of the frame shows the main structure (the "backbone") of a mountain bike. The bicycle manufacturer (who usually builds only the frame) adds all the other components and accessories—these are supplied by other companies. The main frame is made from thick metal tubes, consisting of the top tube, the seat tube, the down tube, and the head tube, and thinner tubes for the rear triangle, consisting of the seat stays and the chain stays. The size of the frame (or the length of the seat tube) determines the overall size of the bicycle.

Compared to other bicycles, the mountain bike's frame is stronger and more rigid, and it also differs in its dimensions. The individual tubes usually have a larger diameter than those used for other bicycles. These tubes give the mountain bike greater torsion strength, guaranteeing stable steering ability on uneven road surfaces, even during high-speed riding. Mountain bike frames made from particularly thick tubes are usually called "oversized" frames. Today many manufacturers use aluminum tubes. These tubes are either welded together or connected by gluing internal lugs to the inside, at the end of the tubes.

Using aluminum tubes, however, does not greatly reduce the bike's overall weight. Although aluminum has less density, it

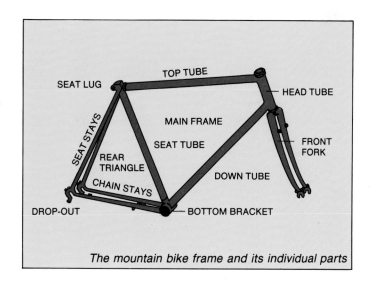

The mountain bike frame and its individual parts

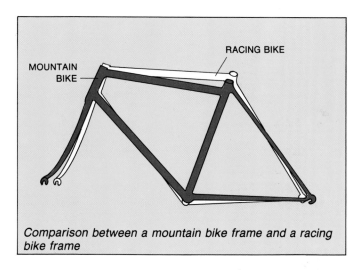

Comparison between a mountain bike frame and a racing bike frame

is also considerably weaker and less rigid than steel-alloy tubes of comparable thickness. Aluminum tubes must be considerably thicker than steel-alloy tubes when used for mountain bike frames.

The dimensions of a mountain bike can best be compared to those of a conventional utility bicycle. Some competition models with much more "aggressive" geometry have dimensions and tube angles that are closer to those of a racing bike. The bottom diagram on page 17 compares a mountain bike and a typical racing bike. The differences can be summed up as follows:

- The distance between the bottom bracket and the ground is increased by about 1″ for better ground clearance. This lessens the chance of the chain rings hitting or getting caught on off-road obstacles such as tree trunks or rocks.

- The mountain bike's top tube is lower than one on a regular bike, giving the rider as much legroom as possible, and allowing the rider to get his saddle in a very low position for downhill riding.

- The angle of the head tube is shallower on the mountain bike, allowing for better shock absorption and greater steering stability.

- The clearances between the frame and the wheels are greater on a mountain bike, so that the wide tires can move freely, even when the ground is muddy and soft.

Steering

The drawing below shows the steering components. The front fork is connected to the frame with the bearings of the headset. The handlebars are connected to the fork via an adjustable stem.

The flat, straight, and generally rather wide handlebars are one of the characteristics of the mountain bike. This design, however, has more to do with looks than with practicality. The mountain bike handles best when the width of the handlebars does not exceed 22″ (55 cm) and when the ends are angled slightly back (approximately 7–10°). The ends should be fitted with pliable but sturdy hand grips.

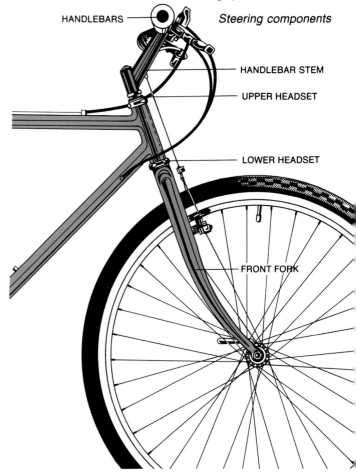

HANDLEBARS

Steering components

HANDLEBAR STEM

UPPER HEADSET

LOWER HEADSET

FRONT FORK

Typical mountain bike steering system: long handlebar stem, wide handlebars, and high-quality headset

Saddle and Seat Post

The saddle is attached to the frame through a seat post with a binder bolt. The mountain bike is equipped with a quick-release mechanism which allows for easy height adjustment of the saddle (see the drawing below). The saddle should be as comfortable as possible because it carries more of the rider's weight than it would on a racing bike. Since the mountain bike encounters more severe road conditions than the racing bike, the impact of such conditions is transferred via the saddle to the rider.

The best saddles are made from leather with coil springs, like the Brooks ATB model. Other models are filled with a gel-like material. The seat

One fashionable development is a long handlebar stem that forces the biker to lean too far forward. This might be an advantage when using the bike in specific competitions. For normal use, and when the biker will ride for long distances (rather than navigating in slow motion around rock formations) long handlebar stems are a disadvantage. This is particularly true for the woman biker who (generally) has short arms relative to the length of her legs. A shorter handlebar allows for a much more comfortable riding position. If the handlebars seem too long for your reach, replace the standard stem with a shorter version.

The handlebar stem is attached to the front fork with an expander bolt with a wedge or cone, clamping the stem tightly into the front fork. The stem must be inserted up to the mark. If there is no mark, make one with an indelible-ink marking pen at the point where at least 2½" (65 mm) of the stem is inserted in the tube. A clamped sleeve attaches the handlebars to the handlebar stem. A double or "V"-shaped stem extension gives the rider somewhat less legroom when getting out of the saddle while going down a steep incline. However, the advantage is more safety in case of an accident.

Saddle and seat post

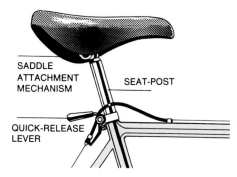

SADDLE ATTACHMENT MECHANISM

SEAT-POST

QUICK-RELEASE LEVER

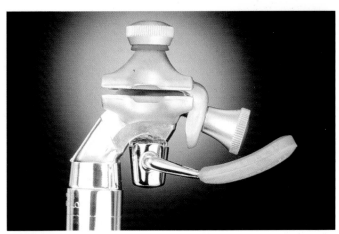

A wonderful seat post with a quick-release mechanism and an Allen-head adjustment bolt.

post must be at least 12″ (30 cm) in length, considerably longer than is necessary for conventional bikes, because more height adjustments are necessary. The seat post should also have a mark. Beyond this mark an extension of the post is unsafe. A good-quality mountain bike has a seat post made from an aluminum alloy and it also has an easy-to-adjust mechanism for tilting the seat and for horizontal adjustments.

Wheels

Thick, deep-tread tires are another characteristic of the mountain bike. As shown on page 21, each wheel consists of a hub, a network of spokes, a rim, and a tire with an inner tube—the same as on any other bike. Mountain bike wheels are much stronger, yet they're remarkably light.

When compared to the conventional American utility bike, they are similar in size—outer diameter of 26″ (650 mm) and a width of 1.75 to 2.125 inches. However, thanks to the very specific construction of rim and tire, the mountain bike's wheels are much more robust and the tires tolerate much higher air pressure. Increased tire pressure creates less rolling resistance on firm ground, and also protects the tire, inner tube, and rim against damage.

Tires come in many different treads, the choice of which will depend on the type of terrain a biker intends to ride on. A new variation of the mountain bike has recently made its appearance: the "hybrid," with tires that are not quite as thick as the mountain bike's. The tire sizes for this bike, either 700 × 35 or 650 × 35 are French sizes—(ISO 35-622 and 35-584 respectively). These tires also tolerate high air pressure and have a less pronounced tread than the mountain bike's. Since these tires have to be mounted on a different rim, you cannot use tires from the mountain bike.

The inner tube is inflated using a valve. The drawing on page 21 shows three different types of valves.

The Presta valve is recommended for mountain bikes, because it is easier to inflate than either of the other two types. The easiest way to inflate a bike tire with a Schrader valve is with an air compressor at a gas station, set at the proper pressure. CO_2 cartridge inflators are also used, as well as the conventional hand pump.

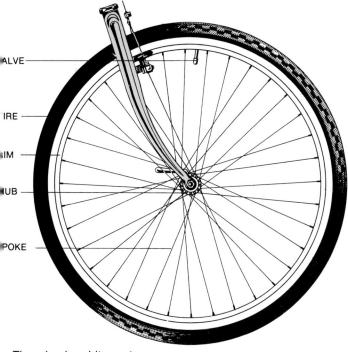

VALVE

TIRE

RIM

HUB

SPOKE

The wheel and its parts

front fork that are supposed to guard against unintentional front-wheel release. In practice, however, it means that the advantages of the quick-release mechanism have been lost, because the lock nut has to be loosened every time the wheel is to be removed or remounted.

Drivetrain

The drivetrain (those components that transfer pedal power to the rear wheel) consists of the

Different types of air valves ▷

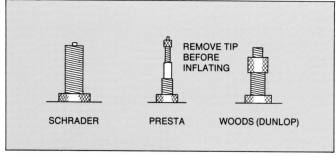

SCHRADER

PRESTA

REMOVE TIP BEFORE INFLATING

WOODS (DUNLOP)

The hub on most high-quality mountain bikes is attached to the wheel with a quick-release mechanism. An axle-nut attachment is by no means a sign of inferior construction. On the contrary, it has its advantages. The axle is not hollow, and it's therefore sturdier, provided it is of superior quality, in which case each nut is fitted with integral washers. A fashionable, and rather annoying invention is the use of drop-outs on the

"Ground Control Extreme"

"Crossroads" for riding on firm surfaces

"Ground Control" for difficult terrain

21

pedal, the crank arm, the bottom bracket, the chain rings, the chain, and the freewheel with sprockets. These parts are closely associated with the gearing mechanism, which is discussed separately.

Mountain bikes are generally built with high-quality components that were adapted from those for racing bikes. With mountain bikes, the design takes into consideration the special needs of off-road riding. For instance, the pedals are built to prevent the feet from slipping off too quickly; they're constructed with sealed ball bearings which guard against penetrating dirt or moisture. Sealed bottom brackets are chosen for the same reason. At one point it was fashionable to use noncircular chain rings. The trend (set by the Shimano Company) began with the rhombus-shaped chain rings of the Bio-Pace version. Other companies introduced elliptical chain rings. It was believed that these designs would be advantageous to the novice biker. The aim was to lengthen the power phase and thereby save energy by pulling the crank arm more quickly through the "dead" point. However, after attaining a sufficient speed, round chain rings are (if anything) more efficient. The mountain bike, in particular, has no problems because of its low gear ratio. Today, most high-quality mountain bikes are again built using round chain rings.

Derailleur Gears

There are two types of gearing systems: derailleur gears and hub gears. Mountain bikes are equipped exclusively with derailleur gears. See the drawing on page 22.

The derailleur moves the chain laterally in order to advance into a different gear. The mountain bike uses a triple front

Drivetrain components

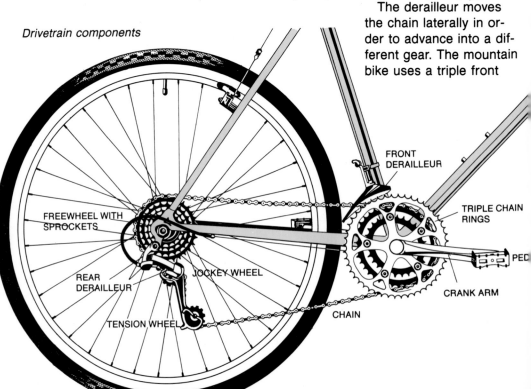

FRONT DERAILLEUR

TRIPLE CHAIN RINGS

FREEWHEEL WITH SPROCKETS

PED

REAR DERAILLEUR

JOCKEY WHEEL

CRANK ARM

TENSION WHEEL

CHAIN

Handlebars with STI integral gear lever and brake lever by Shimano

Rear derailleur with a protective device

chain ring and a 6- or 7-sprocket freewheel on the rear wheel. This (in theory) adds up to 18 or 21 gears, respectively. Shifting is surprisingly easy with gear levers mounted on the handlebars, that are, in turn, connected to the derailleur by a bowden cable.

Chapter 5 discusses in detail all the pertinent information concerning gear-shifting.

Some city bikes come with hub gears. The 5-speed hub gear from Fichtel & Sachs or from Sturmey-Archer are the best known. Both are now available with drum

brakes, or without brakes altogether, in which case normal rim brakes can be installed. Because of wide-range gearing, the hub gearshift system is well-suited to riding in mountainous terrain. On the other hand, the hollow axle reduces the stability of the hub.

Brakes

Brakes come in two different versions: caliper brakes and hub brakes. Mountain bikes are almost exclusively equipped with caliper brakes, and many different varieties are available. Regardless of type, all brakes are operated from a handlebar-mounted lever connected by a flexible bowden cable. The three most common brake systems are shown at the right.

Most mountain bikers prefer cantilever brakes—the same brakes that were in use in the first days of the mountain bike. Excellent brake leverage allows the rider to stop his bike even on a steep decline. A special model of this type is the self-activating version produced by Wilderness Trails and SunTour. Here a portion of the energy created by the moving wheel increases the pressure of the brake pads against the rim.

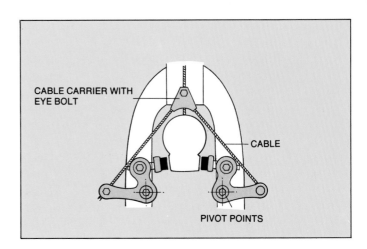

Cantilever brake

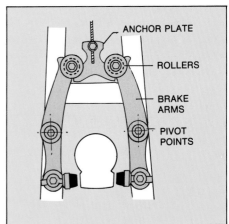

Brake with anchor plate

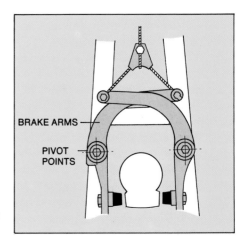

U-brakes

24

The cantilever is the most commonly used brake type.

ride—nothing rattles, nothing comes loose, nothing gets in your way—some accessories can be useful under certain circumstances. For off-road riding, only a battery-operated lighting system is recommended.

Some of the standard accessories for other bikes cannot be mounted easily on a mountain bike because of the mountain bike's greater tube diameters and because of the increased vibration the bike is subject to when riding off-road. Make sure that the accessories you want are designed specifically for a mountain bike, as described in detail in chapter 4.

Accessories

Here we'll cover "normal" accessories, as well as those items designed specifically for the mountain bike: derailleur-, and chain-protector guards, as well as Hite-Rites (adjusting-spring mechanisms for the saddle). Although a bike with the minimum number of accessories is a joy to

3
The Right Mountain Bike

Choosing a mountain bike—the fun should last as long as the bike does

Not every mountain bike is the same. Indeed, there are great differences between different models. Size and design can vary greatly. Where you might want to ride your bike might make one bike more suited than another. This chapter will help you decide which mountain bike is best for your needs. This is of special importance when buying a new bike. Even if you already own a mountain bike, you might find some useful hints and suggestions here.

In addition to the "real" mountain bike, there are also hybrids, and mountain touring bikes, both of which are less extreme versions of the mountain bike, with less pronounced tire treads and narrower handlebars. The handlebars sometimes resemble those on racing bikes or sport bikes.

These bikes, while not quite as good as the mountain bike for open-road riding, are, nevertheless, wonderful for daily use and will perform well even under heavy loads.

Which Bike and for What Purpose?

Each bike, including all the mountain bike models, has its own strengths. The choice of bike therefore, depends on its projected use. A bike purchased for one particular activity can just

Whether you're a racer or a leisure cyclist, you'll find a bike that suits your needs.

27

Small compact frame with angled top tube

Competition frame with oversized aluminum tubes

as well be used for something else. This is particularly true for the normal mountain bike. It is as good a bike for off-road riding as it is for a leisurely outing, or for commuting. If you have one or several bikes, your choice should be governed by what the bike's most frequent use will be. Most models come in a variety of different types that, to the casual observer, look very much the same but differ greatly in price. Quality of true mountain bikes differs so greatly that it's difficult to recommend one over another. Some manufacturers build only very high-quality bikes while others build only very inexpensive bikes. Others specialize and build only one particular type. In general, however, manufacturers offer a wide range of models, from the very inexpensive to the very expensive—from the very simple city bike to the heavy-duty mountain bike. Many manufacturers have become specialists in mountain bikes. They are, for the most part, located in the United States and the Far East and have more recently made their way into the European market as well. They are not necessarily better or worse than other, lesser known brand names. The bike shopper should not necessarily look only for a particular make. The decision should be made according to the following criteria:

- Type
- Equipment
- Quality
- Price
- Size.

First decide (with the help of what we've just discussed) which type of bike best suits your needs. Take into consideration not only the bike's primary use, but also how much of a load you want your bike to carry. You might be totally justified buying a full-fledged mountain bike for occasional demanding use, even if you spend

A European mountain bike "descendant": equipped with narrower tires and practical accessories—for touring and as a city bike

A "lady's version" of a cross between a mountain bike and a sports bike

90% of your time riding on asphalt pavement. Which bike you choose will depend on your personal circumstances, taste, and preference. These factors by no means stay constant over time. Today you may lean towards one particular model, while in a few years you may be intrigued by something altogether different. Remember, you can always equip your bike later to suit your newfound interest.

With the appropriate accessories, and the required adaptations in your riding technique, almost any bike can be used for multiple purposes.

After you've gathered the necessary information about the model of your choice, consider the different equipment being offered and see if the accessories you'd like will fit that particular model. Accessories for some of the aluminum bikes with oversize tubing have to be custom-designed if they are to fit properly. For instance, check if the bike you've chosen has the eyelets and bosses ("braze-ons") necessary for mounting a particular item. Decide in advance which of the many accessories offered will really serve your needs.

Price and Quality

The quality of any bike can best be determined by its price tag. In general, you get what you pay for, almost never more. Sometimes you might pay more for a manufacturer's name; that can only be justified if behind the name you find expert customer service, or an assurance that all of the parts mounted on the bike are of corresponding quality and are easy to replace. In general, quality within a particular price range won't differ much. Some first-time mountain bike buyers seem to balk at the prices charged for high-quality mountain bikes, although they wouldn't think twice about paying a great deal of money for a wrist-watch. They can't accept that a good mountain bike is seldom available for under $600.00 and a high-end model not for under $1000.00. Certain custom bikes can cost as much as $3000.00.

Before you dismiss a bike as being too expensive and decide to buy a cheaper model, take a good look at the prices for high-quality *parts*. It is more economical to buy a more expensive bike than it is to upgrade a cheap model. Even after replacing all the components on a cheap model, you'll still have (as far as the frame is concerned) an inferior bike.

The quality of a bike can be determined by examining the workmanship, easily seen by inspecting how the individual parts have been joined together. The frame should show clean, precise joints. The bike should have an even, smooth coat of paint, and the aluminum-alloy parts should be free of scratches and grooves. Competent dealers will be able to point all this out to you, but some-

times even they are not capable of recognizing a high-quality mountain bike. Bikes (even those that look like mountain bikes) can be purchased not only from bicycle dealers but also from mail-order houses and cash-and-carry outlets, all offering them for very little money. Don't be fooled. Advice, the ability to test-drive, service, and the availability of replacement parts are important factors when buying a mountain bike. Buying from one of these outlets, often a place with untrained personnel, could prove to be a bad bargain.

Size of the Mountain Bike

The size of the bike is as important as the kind and the quality. If you want it to perform to its optimal potential, consider your bike as a piece of equipment, custom-fitted to your body. High-quality models (true mountain bikes, hybrids, or mountain-touring bikes) are all built in many different sizes.

Mountain bikes come

with 26″ wheels, some are even smaller. However, these wheels may actually be larger than those on other models, due to the extreme thickness of their tires. The standard for the wheels of a true mountain bike is 26 × 1.75 (47-559) to 26 × 2.125 (54-559), meaning that the tires are from 47 to 54 mm wide, and fit a rim bed with a diameter of 559 mm. The mountain touring bike usually has the same measurements, while the hybrid's tires are often somewhat larger in diameter, but narrower in cross section. In general, the wider the tire, the better the off-road performance. Narrower tires with increased air pressure move much more efficiently on pavement.

The size of the frame must be coordinated with the height of the rider. Here is a simple rule of thumb to determine the quality of a bike: a high-quality bike should be available in many different sizes. Even if the dealer does not have every size in stock, it should be easy for him to order the right size from the manufacturer.

The length of the seat tube determines the size

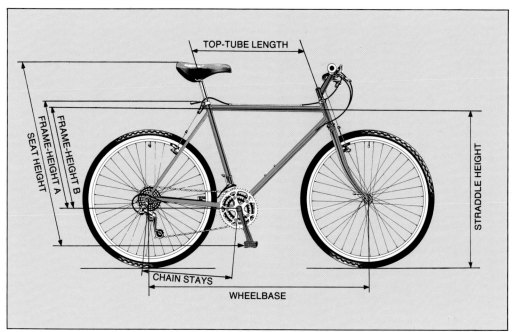

The most important bike measurements. Frame size depends upon the length of the biker's legs

of a bike (see the drawing above) and bike size must correspond to the length of the biker's legs (see the drawing to the right). Mountain bikes are usually measured according to the "French" method (in the drawing above: frame-height B) where the distance between the middle of the bottom bracket and the middle of the top tube represents the height of the frame. The "English" method (frame-height A), on the other hand, uses the distance between the center of the bottom bracket and the top of the seat lug as a measure of frame height.

Measuring frame size for a woman's bike, of course, must be done using the "English" method, because of the way the top tube is mounted on a woman's bike.

The photo on page 32 shows a simple method of checking a mountain bike's proper fit. Lift the front wheel off the ground at least 6-7

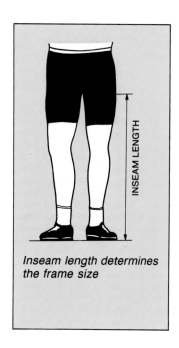

Inseam length determines the frame size

Lifting the front wheel to check the proper frame size

Sometimes other components are also adapted to the body measurements of the biker. A bike with the proper seat-tube height may be too short for some, or too long for others. If you're in doubt, choose the smaller bike. It is possible to add to the overall length by installing a longer handlebar stem. In this way you'll establish the proper handlebar-saddle distance.

inches (15-18 cm), or 4-5 inches (10-13 cm) for a hybrid or touring bike, while standing over the top tube directly in front of the saddle, without the space between your legs and the top tube feeling "crowded." The table on page 121 shows that the frame for a mountain bike is considerably smaller than what is customary for other bicycle types. The reason: the seating position is different for different bicycles and the bottom bracket on a mountain bike is higher. Sometimes it's even necessary to lower the saddle even further so that the feet of the biker can reach the

ground when riding off-road.

If the bike you like is not in stock in the proper size, look for a bike that is almost correct and determine how much bigger or smaller your bike should be. You could also try a model from another manufacturer that fits you. If both manufacturers measure frame sizes by the same method, you'll then be able to order the right size bike from your preferred manufacturer.

The bike industry has established standard sizes. A particular frame size will have corresponding seat-tube and top-tube lengths.

Custom-Made Mountain Bikes

Very special mountain bikes (we're talking about models where the price of the "bare" frame is $1000.00 and up) are sometimes custom-made. Such bikes are made by special frame builders. They're not worth the money unless you've gained considerable biking experience and you can tell the bike maker precisely what it is that you want. It is not enough to know the size and the geometry of the frame, and the material you want. You must also be able to choose all the other parts that you need.

It is possible to choose just those parts to suit your particular needs, and then either mount them to the frame yourself, or have somebody do it for you. This is a very expensive undertaking. The connoisseur might not mind just as long as he can have exactly what he wants, rather than owning an "off-the-rack" model.

Women's Bikes

Except for small women, I recommend a mountain bike with a straight top tube. The size will be correct with the saddle lowered so that the rider can touch the ground with both feet. The rider should be able to comfortably reach the handlebars with both the saddle and the handlebars at the same height.

Sometimes the frame of a man's bike is too large for many women (and for some smaller men, too). In such cases, only a custom-made

How the bike will be used should determine the choice of model. Here's a competition mountain bike.

A sturdy woman's bike. Important detail: extra stays between the seat stays and the chain stays

frame or a specific woman's model will fit.

The best frame for a woman's bike (shown in the photo above) has a single large-diameter top tube joining the seat tube and additional stays, connecting the rear wheel axle and the seat tube at the same point. This construction is by far the best of any woman's bike available.

Women's bikes, however, have other, special features. It is not simply a matter of lowering the top tube and making the overall bike a little smaller. Generally, women are not just shorter than men. A female's pelvis is wider

than a man's, and, taking the overall size of the body into consideration, a woman's legs are longer, her torso shorter, her shoulders narrower, and her arms shorter.

A bike bought "off the rack" seldom allows for all these considerations. A few manufacturers take the trouble to properly design mountain bikes for women. Such bikes should have the following: a special saddle (wider than normal), and (in relation to the height) a relatively short frame and narrower handlebars with a shorter stem.

Women's saddles, similar to racing saddles (only considerably wider

in the back and with more padding), are produced by several manufacturers. If the bike you choose does not have such a saddle, ask the dealer to exchange it. Do this at the time of purchase so that you will only have to pay the price difference between the two saddle models.

Used Bikes

As a result of the mountain bike's rapid development, a flourishing trade in used bikes has developed. Someone, somewhere wants to exchange his two-year-old model

This is mountain biking, too.

for a newer, "up-to-date" version. This is good news for you, if you don't care for the latest trends and all the latest in paraphernalia.

The bikes from just a few years ago are by no means useless or bad today. On the contrary: some features found on earlier mountain bikes have reappeared on the very latest models.

If you are considering a used bike, beware if the bike is really inexpensive. The bike might be stolen. Ask for proof—a receipt, or a guarantee—that shows that the bike was honestly acquired. Make a note of the serial number (located under the bottom bracket or on a rear drop-out). Check with local police to see if a bike with that serial number was reported stolen. If the bike was not stolen, check carefully to see what shape the bike in in. Make sure that everything you expect to be there is in place and in good condition. Distortion in the frame tubing, improper functioning of the drivetrain, or the derailleur, or the brakes, loose steering and wobbly pedals are all signs that the bike has not been well maintained. Fixing these problems might be expensive.

Determining the saddle height. With the leg slightly bent, the heel should reach the pedal at its lowest point.

Saddle and Handlebar Positions

Even a well-chosen bike does not always fit its rider's body. The saddle and the handlebars must be adjusted to assure a comfortable ride. Certain situations require adjustments: riding downhill requires the saddle to be lower and farther back than when climbing uphill or riding on level ground. See also chapter 6.

For the basic seat position, check both drawings shown on this page. The saddle height is correct when the rider's heel reaches the pedal with the pedal in its lowest position. The forward position is correct if the rider's knee is vertically in line with the axis of the pedal, when the crank arm is horizontal in a forward position. In general,

the handlebars and the saddle should be at the same level. For riding in traffic, however, raise the handlebars by about 1¼" (3 cm) for a better view of traffic.

Almost as important as the seat height is the horizontal distance between the saddle and the handlebars. This distance

is almost always too long on today's bikes, forcing the rider to lean too far forward. This awkward position is only an advantage under such extreme conditions as riding downhill in very rough terrain. Over time, this position is terribly tiring. Remedy this by exchanging the handlebar stem

Knee is positioned vertically over the axle of the pedal: The crank arm is in a horizontal, forward position

for a shorter one. The shorter stem requires a bit of manual dexterity to install, but you can do it, following the instructions in chapter 10. You could also ask a mechanic to do it for you. The same advice applies to adjusting the width of the handlebars. If they're too wide, saw off the ends so that the handlebars measure no more than 22″ (55 cm).

The necessary adjustments that you'll encounter most often are easy to do, and are described in detail in the following paragraphs.

Saddle adjustment is easy with the help of the quick-release mechanism.

SADDLE-HEIGHT ADJUSTMENT

A mountain bike is usually equipped with a quick-release mechanism—no tools are necessary.

1. To release the mechanism, turn the lever.
2. Move the saddle (with the seat post) to its required height.
3. Return the lever to its original position.

If moving the lever is difficult, loosen the locknut (on the other side) by one or two turns, with the lever in the open position.

Saddle adjustment using an Allen wrench

SADDLE-POSITION ADJUSTMENT

To move the saddle into the new position, loosen the bolt that holds the saddle to the seat post. The necessary tool is an appropriate wrench, usually an Allen wrench.

1. Determine to what degree and in which direction the adjustment has to be made.
2. Loosen the bolt until the saddle can be easily moved.
3. Bring the saddle into the desired position, holding it securely in that position while you tighten the bolt.

Some mountain bikes have a saddle support that looks like an upside-down "L" and it is, in turn, equipped with another quick-release mechanism. It allows you to adjust the saddle backwards or forward.

ADJUSTING HANDLEBAR HEIGHT

This adjustment requires an Allen wrench that fits the expander bolt at the top of the handlebar stem.

1. Loosen the expander bolt, tapping lightly to loosen the wedge, if necessary.

Loosening the expander bolt to adjust the handlebar height

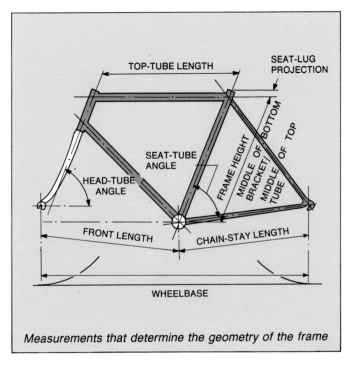

Measurements that determine the geometry of the frame

38

2. Bring the handlebars into proper position, and hold them in that position as you tighten the expander bolt.

Mountain Bike Geometry

Here we mean how the geometric design of the frame affects the performance (steering) of a bicycle. See the drawing on page 38.

Some basic knowledge of this "geometry" theory is necessary when choosing the proper mountain bike. In the beginning, mountain bikes were designed for off-road downhill riding; the frame geometry was based on the construction of the Schwinn Excelsior, a bike first built around 1933. The result was a rather long bike with a long wheelbase, and shallow angles of the head tube and the seat tube relative to the horizontal top tube. The typical measurements were: wheelbase—43" (110 cm); chain-stay length—19" (48 cm); seat-tube angle—70°, and head-tube angle 65°.

After many changes, a bike emerged that had greater maneuverability and climbing ability. The measurements are still being used by most of the leading bike manufacturers. The wheelbase and the chain stays are relatively short (wheelbase no more than 41½", chain stays no more than 17¾"), and the angles are 73° for the seat tube and 70° for the head tube.

Special bike for use on rocky terrain and "observed trials": small wheels, long wheelbase, and very low gear ratios

4
Accessories and Clothing

A mountain bike alone does not make a mountain biker; you'll still need a few accessories for the bike and the biker.

The sensible biker won't buy everything that he sees offered for his mountain bike.

Most mountain bikes and hybrids are "stripped" when they reach the dealer's showroom. If such a bike is what you want—wonderful. It's great fun to experience how light and silent a bike really is in its purest form.

Yet, there will be times when it will rain; or it will get dark before you get home; or you will have to park your bike somewhere where you can't watch it; or you'll want to take something with you that's too big to fit in your pockets. In such cases you'll need some of the following: mudguards, lights, a lock, and luggage racks.

Some accessories are used constantly; they may be simple, practical, or just plain nice to have. A water bottle and an electronic speedometer are two examples. A pump and a tire-repair kit should be taken with you wherever you go.

Some items are specifically designed for the mountain bike: spring-adjusting mechanisms for the saddle, or protective devices for the chain wheels and for the derailleur. Decide now which accessories are necessary for your particular circumstances, and if the bike you are buying is suited to them.

Not everything is as practical as some manufacturers would have you believe. Don't hesitate to remove what seems to be impractical. Pay attention to installation instructions (if they're included). Even if parts are already on the bike when you buy it, ask the dealer to get the instructions for you, if he doesn't have them. This is particularly important for relatively complicated items—like the speedometer (bicycle computer).

General Equipment and Accessories

Not every piece of equipment will fit every type of bike. Fenders, for example, are made in several different widths. Some mountain bike frames are so small that there is no room for even the smallest fenders.

Accessories need care, particularly the moving parts, and they need to be cleaned, lubricated, and adjusted, like every other part of the bike. As far as mounting is concerned, those parts that are only secured on one point will loosen quickly.

Fasten everything (at least) at two points, even if the manufacturer does not suggest that you to do so. Loose bolts should be tightened immediately.

Those parts that are mounted directly on the frame will stay in place much better if a patch (as used to repair a damaged inner tube) is attached to the frame first. First, clean the frame tube and coat it with rubber solution on the spot

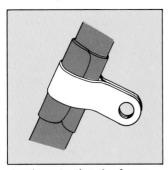

Patch protecting the frame tube

where the item is to be mounted, just as you would when repairing an inner tube. Let the solution dry and attach a patch to the frame tube. If you need a big patch, make one yourself from an old inner tube. If you make it yourself, clean the patch, spread rubber solution on it and allow it to dry for at least three minutes.

Luggage Racks

Most high-quality luggage racks are of welded aluminum or steel, with triangulated supports, although a few models are made of tubular material. Steel rod should be at least ¼″ (6 mm), aluminum of at least 5/16″ (8 mm). The mounting bolts must be checked regularly and, if necessary, tightened or replaced.

The stays of the rack are attached directly to eyelets on the drop-out, which means under those for the fender and not above (if they are mounted to the same eyelet). Also, washers are absolutely necessary when mounting this equipment. The connection at the seat stay must also be very secure. Generally, the use of a separate clamp may be the best solution.

Fenders

Special mountain bike fenders are also available. They are wider than those made for regular bikes. It has been my experience that the simple, plastic clip-on guards are much better than the permanently installed types

(made of either metal or plastic). Permanently installed fenders are attached to the frame with stays.

The bolts that connect the stays to the fender and the drop-out need occasional tightening. If the fender becomes twisted or touches the wheel, the bolts with which the stays are mounted can be loosened, the stays either pulled further out or in, and the bolt tightened again.

Usually eyebolts are used. The diagram below illustrates how the parts are installed. If you use a simple bolt, use a washer under the nut as well as between the stays and the head of the bolt.

Installing the fender stays

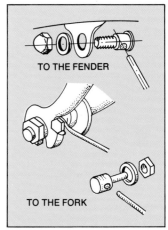

TO THE FENDER

TO THE FORK

A fully equipped mountain touring bike. Only a front reflector is missing.

Kickstand

The kickstand, once widely used on utility bikes, is not very practical on a mountain bike. It often comes loose and then rubs against the wheel or the crank arm when it's retracted, and then it won't support the bike when parked. These problems can be eliminated or prevented by regularly tightening the mounting bolt. An 8 mm Allen wrench is a good investment, even if this is its only use. If the bike cannot be properly parked, shorten the kickstand using a hacksaw. However, so-called double-leg kickstands are available—they balance the bike much better. This kickstand is also installed at the stays, using either an 8 mm Allen wrench (for bikes with flat connecting plates on the chain stays), or using a hexagonal bolt and nut.

When using the bike primarily off-road, the only type of kickstand to use is the one mounted at the rear wheel. This keeps the bike upright and the kickstand won't get in the way when riding over obstacles, something that is bound to happen when using the conventional side-, or double-leg kickstand.

Bicycle Computer

For off-road use, the old-fashioned, mechanically driven speedometer is not useful. More and more electronic versions

The bicycle computer is popular and useful.

Pump

A lot of air is needed to inflate the huge tires of a mountain bike. For this reason, purchase a large-volume pump. Choose a pump with a connector that fits the valve of your tire. The model with a connector for the Presta valve also works with the European Woods valve, but not the other way around. Most mountain bikes come with the same Schrader valves that are used on car tires. Be sure you have the proper pump, or use the air hose at the gas station.

Locks

Many different types of bicycle locks are on the market—only a few assure real safety. Not very recently my bike was stolen, although it was securely locked with an adequate lock (an American-made large "U"-shaped lock). I couldn't attach the bike to any fixed object—and the trees in the woods were too thick. The thief just carried away the bike (lock and all) and broke the lock at his leisure. In such a situation a long

are now being offered— "bicycle computers." They work flawlessly.

Choose a model with the fewest buttons and moving parts because when riding your bike, every additional part is one part too many. Follow the manufacturer's instructions for installation.

Warning Devices

Although they're rarely used in the United States, the restrained use of bells or horns can be useful. The bell or horn must be in easy reach of the normal position of the

hand, and it must be attached securely. The bell should be maintained periodically. Remove the cup and apply a drop of oil to the mechanism. If your bell has a hammer mechanism, of course, the above does not apply. If there seems to be a problem, check the cup first to see if it has accidentally come in contact with another part, the brake cable, for instance. If it hasn't, bend the hammer a bit until the bell works properly again. Battery-operated horns are also available— they're much more noticeable, more reliable, and less sensitive than the mechanical models.

cable lock would have been better, although these types are normally more vulnerable. To maintain any lock, I suggest that it should only be oiled very sparingly. This prevents the formation of a mixture of dirt and oil creating a thick mush in the lock mechanism. A few drops of oil in the keyhole and where the shackle enters the lock, applied once or twice a year, will usually be sufficient.

Seat Adjuster

This product (a typical accessory for the mountain bike) allows for easy seat-height adjustment. As shown in the photo below, it consists of a spring that is attached at top to the saddle post

"Hite-Rite" seat adjustment mechanism

and at bottom around the binder bolt. The spring keeps the saddle perfectly aligned after each adjustment. The adjustment can be done even while riding the bike. This "Hite-Rite" might also prevent saddle theft.

Adjustment is made by loosening the quick-release and letting the weight of your body change the height. Afterward, the quick-release is tightened again. When mounting (before the spring adjuster is tightened), position the seat about ¾" (2 cm) higher than the maximum height you want. This will keep the spring always under tension, regardless of what height adjustment you make later.

Chain-Ring Protector

The most useful chain-ring protector is the "Rockring," a very strong ring attached to the outer chain ring. Make sure that the "Rockring" does not interfere with the movement of the chains. Another alternative is a chain-ring protector installed directly to the frame, like the one the German mountain-bike

Protection for the rear derailleur

builder Günther Sattler mounts on his bikes.

Derailleur Protection

This device, a simple metal bracket (see the photo above), should be part of every mountain bike. It protects the lower derailleur against damage, and it prevents the right drop-out from getting bent out of shape. If you mount it after you purchase your bike, it is easily attached at the right axle nut or at the quick-release mechanism of the back wheel.

Lights

There are two different types of bike lights available. The first type is the generator-powered light. A battery-operated light is generally more reliable, particularly off-road. When it comes to traffic safety, maintenance of the light system should come first, because no other mechanical failure leads to more accidents than a faulty lighting system.

Generator with its roller in contact with the edge of the rim. This position saves excess wear on the tire.

GENERATOR-POWERED LIGHTS

The generator-powered light consists of the generator, a headlight, and a rear light. The parts are connected by electrical wires. In the passive position, the generator must be mounted with a space of ³⁄₁₆″–⁵⁄₁₆″ (5–8 mm) between the roller and the tire. When in use, the generator must press against the tire securely at the flat portion on the side of the tire. The generator must be aligned with respect to the axle of the back wheel. This can be done easily by loosening the mounting bolt and making the proper alignment. The generator should be mounted on the left side of the rear wheel, pointing forward.

The best generator uses a rubber roller which touches the wheel's rim, rather than the tire sidewall. Its operation is quiet, and it won't slip in rain or snow, because its small rubber roller minimizes the surface area that makes contact with the rigid portion of the wheel, resulting in higher contact pressure. Consequently, the roller (while exerting more pressure) does not create unnecessary drag.

The headlight should be mounted so that the center of the beam falls about 30–50 feet (10–15 m) directly in front of the bike. The headlight bolt should be tight enough so that the light will not slip, but loose enough so that it is still possible to adjust it by hand. For best results, the light should be positioned as high as possible on the bike. The rear light should not be attached to a fender. The vibrations (characteristic of off-road cycling) increase the stress on the fender with the additional weight of the light, and breakage could occur easily. Good places for mounting the headlight are the seat stays or the luggage-rack stays. The mounting bolt can be easily connected to the metal portion of the frame.

Make sure you have a replacement bulb with

48

you when you go on trips. Wrap it in tissue paper and store it in the repair kit to avoid breakage. Some systems include storage space for the replacement bulbs. In general, generator systems use a 6v, 2.4 watt bulb (0.4 amp) for the headlight. Halogen bulbs of the same rated output produce more light, last longer and don't lose their intensity as fast as regular bulbs. Since halogen bulbs have a special base, they can only be used on fixtures made specifically for them.

Generator mounted to the underside of the chain stay. Not recommended for bikes used for hard off-road riding.

BATTERY-OPERATED LIGHTING SYSTEMS

Only battery-operated lights are really suitable for off-road use. A truly efficient battery lighting system must have two mono-cell batteries (the big cylindrical types), and it should use 2.4 volt bulbs. Since batteries have a limited life, check the headlights once a week, even if the lights are not in use. To prevent damage caused by weather or vandalism, remove the lights whenever you're not using them.

Don't forget to remount them when you know that you might be riding in the dark. Carry replacement batteries and bulbs. In case of malfunction (in addition to checking the bulb and the batteries), check the electrical contact points,

The front reflector

sand them lightly and then apply battery grease (available in tubes in auto supply stores). Rechargeable NiCad batteries should be completely drained before you start the recharging process. If necessary, purposely leave the lights on to

"kill" the battery before recharging.

REAR REFLECTORS

Rear reflectors are a secondary light source. They reflect all the light that hits them. Reflectors becomes less effective when the inside of the plastic becomes damp. Replace reflectors immediately when they crack or break.

Clothing

Although you could, conceivably, ride your mountain bike dressed in any outfit you chose, you'd

A boot that meets all the requirements for off-road use

The experience of a mountain bike trip: unpaved roads high in the mountains

50

be much more comfortable, and much safer if you wore clothing specifically designed for off-road riding. Even if you don't want to look like a bike racer, the best and most comfortable clothing is designed for a racer's use. The outfits you use for mountain bike riding should retain the comfort of bike-racing clothing, and they should add that extra bit of protection necessary for off-road conditions.

Although mountain bike boots are similar to other cycling shoes, their soles have a deeper tread and are made of a more rigid rubber or synthetic material. A protective strap across the instep prevents shoelaces from catching in the chain. Sturdy soles spread the pedalling over the entire area of your foot's sole, and the deep tread prevents you from slipping when walking.

Biking shorts and pants are made from skintight elasticized material, with an inner lining made of chamois leather that absorbs perspiration and prevents chafing. The long version, with built-in knee pads, is recommended for mountain biking.

Even if you dress conservatively, choose a pair of pants made from skin-tight elasticized material. They won't interfere with riding. If you wear a normal pair of pants, make sure that pant legs are narrow on the bottom, and the right pant leg ought to be tucked into the sock or secured to the leg with a rubber band. All these measures will prevent the pant leg from catching in the chain.

Today's biker's jersey is usually made from skin-friendly man-made material; it's cut exactly like the old bike-racing wool jersey. It is long enough to cover the kidney area even if the rider should be in an extreme forward position. The skintight material won't billow while you're riding, creating an air barrier between the jersey and the body. This barrier keeps the body warm at low temperatures and cool when it's hot. The air barrier regulates the body temperature no matter what the outside temperature or the level of activity might be—as you can clearly feel either when climbing uphill or coasting downhill.

For mountain bike rid-

ing, especially when it's cold, the long-sleeved jersey is recommended. It also provides protection against tree branches. These jerseys come in many brilliant colors, and sometimes they're even tasteful. Those who really don't want to wear these bike-racing jerseys can wear long T-shirts or close-fitting shirts or jerseys. You might miss out on the rather practical rear pocket which is part of the racing jersey. During the winter months, wear a wool jersey rather than a jersey made from man-made fibres.

A cloth cap does not protect the skull as well as a helmet does, but it will protect the scalp, forehead, eyes, and neck against sunburn, a particularly important concern during the summer months. Be sure the cloth fits tight on your head so that the wind can't blow it off.

The traditional, fingerless gloves that racers use are also very practical (in a limited sense) for mountain bike riding. During the winter months, use gloves similar to those worn by cross-country skiers. True bicycling gloves are padded in the palm area. These gloves are useful in spills. They also absorb some of the vibration when you ride over rough surfaces, especially during a fast descent when you have to hold on tight to the handlebars. It's only a matter of time until gloves are designed especially for the mountain biker. Socks should also be mentioned, because not every sock is comfortable when riding a mountain bike. Make sure your socks don't have seams around the toe area—the seams could be bothersome in tight-fitting boots or shoes. Depending upon the weather, wear either wool or cotton socks.

Safety Clothing

Statistics concerning ordinary traffic accidents for bicyclists are frightening. Don't overlook the dangers that also lurk away from "normal" road traffic. Mountain biking has its share of serious accidents, almost always the result of a spill. Only those who have total control of a mountain bike can hope to avoid them. Protect yourself with the proper equipment—a helmet, padded gloves, and pants with knee pads. Energy-absorbing helmets should be worn by every self-respecting mountain biker. In 70% of all fatal bicycle accidents, the biker died of head injuries. These injuries could have been prevented if the biker had simply worn a helmet.

In a typical fatal accident, the rider falls head-first to the ground or his head hits an immovable obstacle. This causes the brain to be thrown against the inside of the cranium. Such an impact results in a sudden retardation, or deceleration, which is expressed in

The helmet on the left is good-looking and safer because it's made in one integral piece.

m/s². The brain is capable of withstanding such an impact if the deceleration does not exceed 3000 m s². At a spill from a bike at 5 ft. (1.50 m) height, a speed of 5 m/s results at the time of impact.

In order to keep deceleration below 3000 m/s² the velocity of the impact has to be reduced to zero in no less than 0.002 seconds. This is achieved by wearing a helmet that establishes an energy-absorbing "crumple-zone" which is created by a layer of rigid foam, approximately ³⁄₄" (2 cm) thick with just enough "give" to avoid exceeding the above-mentioned value. The helmet must be designed to stay on the head during a spill and by itself it should not cause any injuries. A helmet meets these technical criteria if it corresponds to the United States standard ANSI Z-90.4.

Wearing a helmet can reduce by at least 50% the risk of a fatal bicycle accident. Authorities are contemplating the mandatory wearing of helmets. Only when climbing a steep hill in hot weather do I take off my helmet. Perspiration is

Your elbows and your knees need protection, as well as your head.

heavy under such circumstances and air-cooling is almost nonexistent at such low speeds. Wearing a helmet then would become unbearable. Put your helmet back on before you start your descent, because the chance of an accident during the

descent is far greater than during the climb.

Bad-Weather Clothing

Rain and snow are not reasons to leave your bike in the garage, providing your mountain bike is properly equipped and you have the proper protective clothing. Fenders and lights will make your bike rain-, and winter-hardy. The front fender should have a splash guard to protect your feet in the rain. In case you can't find one, it's easy to make one yourself.

The biker should wear airtight clothing that covers the arms and the legs—preferably in several layers. The appropriate clothing is available in bike shops, sporting-goods stores, and camping shops. Choose the individual pieces according to the recommendations already mentioned and make sure the material used is water-repellent. Proper rain clothing depends upon the temperature. A regular biking outfit (of man-made fibres) will do fine if the temperature is not below 60°F, because it doesn't absorb as much rain as wool does. However, when the temperature drops, be sure that you have sufficient protection. Under these conditions, wear warm clothing *and* good rain protection.

Choose a material that both repels water and allows moisture to evaporate. This will wick away

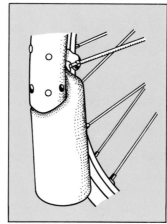
Splash guard for the front fender

body perspiration that develops even during low temperatures. *Goretex* is a most suitable material. However, there are other materials available. The material used for a piece of clothing is important, as is the way the clothing

is cut. It is important that everything fits closely without interfering with movement. Seams should be properly sealed and buttons and zippers should be covered to prevent rain from penetrating.

A rain poncho is more practical than a rain jacket. If the poncho has a hood, don't use it when riding—it will obstruct your view. Instead, wear either a rain hat or a helmet without the air vent. Spats and leggings provide the best protection for your legs. Choose spats—leggings that are open in the back; they will keep your legs dry without being a perspiration trap. Special rain boots designed for cyclists will protect your feet.

Proper rain gear will protect you in many wet situations.

Or, you could use the primitive (but effective) method of putting a plastic bag (the kind used for food storage), over your socks before you put on your shoes.

In cold weather, whether it's raining or not, dress in layers. It's much more effective to wear a shirt and a thin sweater than just one thick wool sweater. A pair of long biking pants under a pair of light wool (or synthetic) pants is much more effective than wearing one thick padded pair of pants. If it gets too hot (when climbing a hill, for example), it's much easier to take off one layer instead of riding in a heavy suit or having to change your whole outfit.

Your extremities should be well protected in really cold weather—fingers, feet, nose, and ears. I have been unable to find a really effective nose protection, but thick (or double-knit) mittens, socks, a cap with flaps that can be pulled over the ears (or separate ear-muffs worn under the cap) will all help to take care of the rest. Boots with an added lining and padded insoles will help keep your feet warm.

Mountain biking is possible in any kind of weather.

5
Handling the Gears

Only those who can shift gears properly will enjoy a mountain bike's advantages

The purpose of the gears is to optimize the ratio between pedalling speed and wheel rotation speed. Rolling resistance and consequently wheel rotation/riding speed depends (greatly) on the terrain. A biker can achieve his best performance with a relatively high pedal speed (80 to 120 revolutions per minute), which is the most gentle and efficient way to use muscles, tendons, and joints. To maintain this speed, select a low gear when the resistance is high, and a high gear when the resistance is low.

Mountain bikes are always equipped with derailleur gears. The derailleur gear on the mountain bike has three different-size chain rings attached to the right-hand crank. At the rear wheel is a freewheel with six or seven different-size sprockets. You can select an appropriate gear for the conditions by using the shift levers mounted on the handlebars. These levers move the chain (via a cable and a derailleur) sideways, so that each time a particular combination of sprocket and chain ring is chosen, you change the transmission ratio. The mountain bike has a particularly wide range of gears. The gear ratio in the lower gears is much lower than on a standard bike, making it possible to climb even the steepest mountain, where you'd normally encounter a high degree of resistance.

Gearing Theory

The ratio between pedal speed and riding speed depends upon the gear that you've engaged. On a bike without a derailleur, with sprocket and the chain rings of the same size, one rotation of the pedal would equal one rotation of the rear wheel. With a typical wheel diameter of 26″ (685 mm) the distance covered by one rotation of the cranks would be 7 ft. (2.1 m). This would add up to 5 mph (7.75 km/h) with a pedal speed of 60 revolutions per minute.

Although that's faster than walking, it's not very fast for a mountain bike. The advantage of biking is that the biker does not have to lift his body weight when rotating the crank arm. A walker lifts his body weight 2½″–3⅛″ (6–8 cm) off the ground with each step. The bicycle affords an important energy savings—energy that's used for the forward motion of the bike. A substantially higher speed, however, can only be achieved if a

57

more effective riding technique is employed.

This can be accomplished if the ratio between the chain ring and the sprockets is such that the rear wheel rotates considerably faster than the crank arms. If the chain ring has 48 teeth, and the sprocket has 16 teeth, the rear wheel will rotate 3 times as fast as the crank arms. When you rotate the crank arm 60 times per minute, you'll reach a speed slightly faster than 14 mph (23 km/h).

Things get a bit more complicated when we consider head wind, gradient, or the surface condition of the road, all the things you'll encounter when mountain biking. Under such circumstances, more energy is needed to navigate the road, while tail winds, downhill, or riding on smooth asphalt in this rather high ratio of 48/16 as mentioned above, can save you much energy. Gearing lets you adjust to any one of the situations you'll encounter. With an equal number of pedal revolutions, the forward movement will be slow in low gear, while in high gear more ground will be covered—provided you

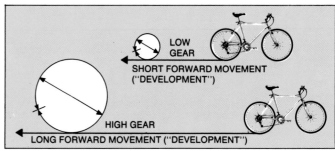

Gear and development—the higher the gear, the longer the development.

have enough energy left in your legs, or you take advantage of a tail wind, or you ride downhill on a smooth surface.

Typically, the lowest gear on a mountain bike has 26 teeth on the chain ring, and 28 teeth on the sprocket. As a result, the rear wheel turns 8% slower than the crank arms. With such a gear you could practically climb a wall. The highest gear has a combination of 46 teeth on the chain ring and 13 teeth on sprocket, so that the rear wheel turns 3.5 times faster than the crank arms. If you're dissatisfied with this arrangement, the information in chapter 10 describes changes that you can make. Although the ratio between the wheel and the crank-arm revolutions is usually expressed in

inches in the United States, it's more logical to identify the ratio according to the distance travelled per crank revolutions, referred to as "development." Development is naturally longer in high gears with a high gear ratio than it is in low gears with a small gear ratio. Development is calculated according to the following formula:

Development = 3.14 × the diameter of the rear wheel × the number of teeth on the chain ring ÷ by the number of teeth on the sprocket. In this case, the diameter of the wheel is expressed in metres.

For a wheel diameter of 26″ (685 mm), the longest and shortest distance would be:

lowest gear: 3.14 × 0.685 × 26 ÷ 28 = 2.1 m

highest gear: 3.14 × 0.685 × 46 ÷ 13 = 7.6 m

Every possible gear position on your mountain bike could easily be determined by using this formula. However, there's an even easier way—use the table on page 119.

In the United States, gears are usually identified by the gear number (in inches). This somewhat archaic method refers to the theoretical number of inches in diameter of the front wheel if it were in a "direct-drive" setup.

To determine inch-gear, use the following formula:

Gear number = the number of teeth on the chain ring × the wheel diameter in inches ÷ the number of teeth on the sprocket.

In terms of gear number, the same combination would work as follows:

lowest gear: 26 × 26 ÷ 28 = 24″

highest gear: 46 × 26 ÷ 13 = 93″

Refer to the table on page 120. You can find the correlation between inch gear and development by using the following formula:

Development (m) = 0.08 × Gear (inch)

Gear (inch) = 12.5 × Development (m)

Gearing Technique

The bicycle's transmission is most efficient when the pedalling rate is rather high. The most efficient rate is 80 rpm, even higher for racing drivers. A certain amount of skill is needed to achieve this. Acquiring this skill is a matter of training. On a ten-speed bike, most people tend to use gears that are too high; however, this isn't always the case for mountain bikes. The mountain bike has such low gears that some people are tempted to use them even on level roads. To overcome that habit, make sure that you gain sufficient ground with each rotation of the crank arm, and that you feel a reasonable resistance.

A system with a triple chain ring and a freewheel with 7 sprockets, in theory, has 21 gears. In reality the extreme

When choosing gears, avoid using the smallest chain ring with the smallest sprocket and the biggest chain ring with the largest sprocket.

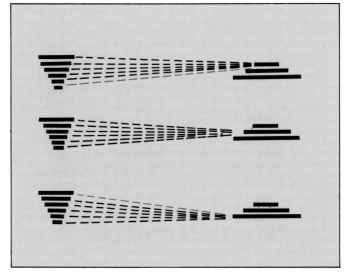

*Handlebar-end shifter
adapted from cyclo-cross*

gears (shown in red on page 59) cannot be used. The angle of the chain of the extreme gears created during shifting interferes either with the derailleur, or the next-larger chain ring or sprocket. In addition, some of the other gears overlap, so that the actual number of available gears is really less than the nominal 18 or 21.

Remember to start out in a low gear, since energy need is considerably greater in that phase than when riding at a constant speed. Shift into a low gear as soon as you slow down for a stop; that will get you into the proper gear for starting again. For several weeks, try to pay attention to the relationship that exists between energy expended, pedalling rate, and riding speed. These observations help you to coordinate your energies with your gearing system.

Shifting Technique

When shifting, try not to apply force to the pedals. Today most derailleur systems are equipped with indexed gearing, where the individual gear positions are synchronized, making shifting gears much easier. First check through all the gears by lifting the bike's rear wheel off the ground and then turning the crank. Observe the change in speed of the rear wheel. Then practise on the road and very consciously go through all the gears. First use the small chain ring in combination with all the sprockets of the freewheel, then do the same with the middle chain ring, and finally use the large chain ring with those sprockets that you think will be of use to you.

When riding on a level, relatively hard road surface or when riding down a gentle downhill slope, use the largest chain ring (controlled by the left shifter) for all gear positions, selecting the appropriate gear with the right lever for the freewheel sprockets. Use the middle chain ring for slight inclines, and the smallest chain ring for steep inclines. If the road surface is soft the very low gears are most efficient; use the middle and the small chain rings.

Changes within each of the three general ranges of gears just described are made only with the rear derailleur. Always get into the appropriate range by selecting the right chain ring before it gets too steep, because shifting becomes almost impossible under the stress of climbing. Practise shifting as long as necessary until you can choose the proper gear automatically.

Over-the-Bar and Under-the-Bar Gear Shifters and Indexed Gearing Systems

Gear-shifting comfort was further improved with the introduction of

The new generation of shifters—independently mounted under-the-bar Shimano shifter, ergonomically well positioned

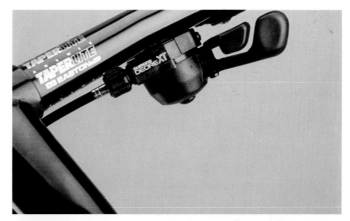

Campagnolo "Bullet-Shifter" integrated in the handlebar grips—shifting without the hand leaving the handlebars

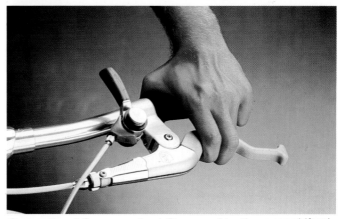

Conventional Campagnolo shifter—combination gear shifter/brake lever

the two-lever "under-the-bar" shifters, which followed the invention of the indexed gearing system, already a considerable improvement over the traditional "friction" method.

The single-lever shifter is mounted on top of the handlebars. Move the right-hand lever one notch forward to select the next-bigger sprocket, backwards to engage the next-smaller sprocket.

The left-hand lever is used to select a bigger or smaller chain ring, by moving it forward or backwards, respectively. Remember this process by visualizing that when shifting into a higher gear both shifters move in a clockwise direction, and counterclockwise when shifting into a lower gear.

The modern two-lever under-the-bar shifters are

mounted on the underside of the handlebars. Your hands never leave the handlebars when you shift gears. Here both shifters have two smaller levers, positioned above each other. The upper lever moves the chain to the next-smaller sprocket, while the lower lever moves the chain to the next bigger one.

However, there are also other models on the market. For instance, Mafac has a wishbone-shaped shifter (also mounted under the handlebars) which is much less complicated—the shifter has two levers that are connected. Campagnolo and Sachs-Huret offer systems that are activated by turning the grips, similar to those used on mopeds and motor scooters. These shifters have 3 positions on the left side and 7 positions on the right.

Adjusting the Gears

You'll need to know how to adjust the gear-shift cable of an indexed gearing system. When the cable connecting the shifter and the derailleur or the chain rings becomes stretched the individual gears won't operate smoothly. You'll hear the chain make dragging noises or the chain will not move from one sprocket or chain ring to another.

Adjusting the shifter (above)

Adjusting the gear system

To correct this problem, you'll have to adjust the cable tension. You'll always find an adjustment mechanism at the gear shifter, and sometimes at the derailleurs too. Tighten the cable slightly whenever the chain no longer moves freely. First, engage the chain in the highest gear.

To tighten the cable, first hold the locknut while turning the adjusting barrel approximately one half-turn counterclockwise. Now go through every gear to see if the chain can be engaged properly and has no slack. If necessary, turn the barrel another quarter-turn and check again. When everything is working properly, hold the adjusting barrel in place and tighten the locknut in a clockwise direction.

6
Handling a Mountain Bike

Smooth pedalling, correct steering, safe braking; proper control increases enjoyment

This chapter examines riding techniques that, once mastered, give you the necessary skills to properly handle your mountain bike. Gear shifting know-how was discussed in the preceding chapter. How to apply the techniques to suit the difficulty of the terrain you might encounter is discussed extensively in chapter 7. You can only take advantage of a mountain bike if you become consciously aware of its unique riding characteristics. Bike riding can be done very skillfully or very clumsily. Here you'll find advice about how to ride in the most comfortable, safest, and most efficient manner.

About 80% of all bikers, including mountain bikers, seem to exert a lot of effort, as is evident when watching their intense facial expressions and the heavy side-to-side swaying of their bodies. They seem to be unsure of themselves, and their progress is slow. Some ride as if the road belonged to them exclusively. Some others pay no attention to other bikers or hikers, and show no consideration.

The experienced bikers not only pedal in a relaxed manner at about twice the speed, they *are* relaxed—even when climbing a hill. When they encounter others, they behave predictably, skillfully, and confidently. They are much less accident-prone. If you follow the advice in this chapter, you will improve your riding habits markedly, and riding will be much less strenuous, no matter what your level of experience is.

Seating Position and Adjustment

Although some people are convinced that a straight upright seating position on a bike is particularly comfortable or healthy, in fact bike riding is more pleasant and easier when your upper body is slightly tilted in a forward position.

Your position on a bike (whether it's a mountain bike or not) can be adjusted to suit any situation. Your position is always based on a rather standard position of the saddle and the handlebars (see the drawing on page 66). Let's assume that the proper bike size has already been chosen (see chapter 3).

First, adjust the height and the position of the seat. The proper height is achieved by loosening

Proper relation between the seat and the handlebars, showing the correct body position, and the correct leg position

the binder bolt. This bolt is usually a quick-release mechanism on a mountain bike. Pull the seat post up to the proper height and refasten the binder bolt. The proper saddle height can be calculated using the following formula:

Seat height = 1.09 × your inseam length (in inches)

Since mountain bike shoes usually have rather thick soles, measure your inseam first without your shoes, and then add the thickness of the sole. If your bike is equipped with special stirrups, add the thickness of these, as well. Measure the correct seat height first by supporting yourself against a doorpost; then adjust the seat so that your leg is almost perfectly straight, with just the slightest knee bend (see the drawing above).

Check the seat-height adjustment by pedalling backwards. If your body sways from side to side in the saddle, your seat is too low.

The clamp bolts that hold the saddle in place may vary from bike to bike but almost all such bolts are designed to adjust both the position and the tilt of the saddle. The top of the saddle is normally in a horizontal position; the knee joint is vertically aligned with the axis of the pedal when the crank arm is in a horizontal position. If the saddle position needs correction, loosen the clamp bolt, tilt the saddle to the desired position and tighten the bolt again. The handlebars should be positioned so that they can be reached

How about a trip over narrow country trails?

comfortably for a prolonged period, and so that the upper body can be lowered without creating undue tension in the back.

Position the handlebars at the start so that the highest point is about ¾″–1½″ (2–4 cm) lower than the saddle. This position should not be changed, even if the saddle is lowered later, and the difference is less or even reversed.

On some mountain bikes, rotating the handlebars slightly will result in a more comfortable body position. Experiment until you find the most comfortable position.

To adjust the handlebar height, loosen the expander bolt. If necessary, tap the stem until the inner wedge (a clamping device inside the stem) loosens, and then bring the handlebars into the proper position and tighten the bolt again.

To adjust the angle of the handlebars, loosen the stem clamp bolts, turn the handlebars in the proper direction and tighten the bolts again.

Riding Style and Bike Control

Even if you practise the right pedalling rate and the proper gear shifting, there is still more that you need to know. You must master steering—it has much to do with how efficient and safe your ride will be. This section pertains more to off-road riding than it does to normal traffic conditions.

67

Tilting the wheel and the handlebars on a curve

the curve and the biking speed. When riding slowly into a tight curve, only a slight tilt is necessary. On the other hand, with the bike tilted only slightly the steering must be more pronounced. Steering is less pronounced or the tilting of the body increases at higher speeds (see the diagram left). Tilting the body is countered when steering the bike in the direction of the tilt. Leaning to the left is compensated by steering to the left, which brings the bike

As a single-track vehicle, the direction a bike travels is not only a function of the handlebars (and by implication the front wheel). The bike also has to be balanced, otherwise centrifugal force would tip the bike over to the outside of the curve. Even when driving straight ahead, a bike continuously maneuvers little curves that are (to a greater or lesser degree) compensated for by adjusting the steering and shifting the body weight.

When negotiating any curve, the degree of tilt of the bike must be coordinated with the radius of

Driving direction for a natural curve (left) and a forced curve (right)

back into its upright position. If you don't quite understand this process, try this maneuver in an empty parking lot or any similar open space.

You can take a curve in either of two ways: naturally (evenly and wide), or forced (abrupt and tight). These methods are depicted in the diagram above. When using the natural method, the biker waits until the bike is tilted in the direction of the curve (for instance to the right, as shown), if he wants to make a right-hand turn. Instead of correcting by also steering to the right, which would shift the body weight and tilt the bike upright again (a necessary reaction when riding straight ahead), remain in a tilted position until you are able to ride through the curve without the bike tipping over. This method is used whenever there is enough space and time to maneuver.

Sometimes, especially off-road, there's neither time nor space to take a curve "naturally." If you suddenly have to avoid an obstacle, you must use the "forced" method. Assume a more pronounced tilted position in the desired direction (leaning into the direction of the curve) then quickly steer in the opposite direction. In order to prepare for a sharp right turn, the biker must temporarily steer to the left. This results in a considerable tilt to the right. Take advantage of this tilt by correcting your steering to the right.

Take time to practise both methods. You really don't have to learn this, because you knew how to do this almost "subconsciously" when you first learned to ride a bike. But, only those who really understand both methods can, if the need

arises, use them con-
sciously and reliably.

Braking Technique

Using brakes properly
must also be practised.
The combined moving
mass of the bike and the
biker represents consid-
erable kinetic energy—
half of the product of the
mass and the riding
speed squared. An im-
pact causes an abrupt,
sudden transfer of this
energy, resulting in con-
siderable damage—either
to the bike, the biker, or
to the object with which
the biker collides. To un-
dertake a change in di-
rection, a bike must often
be slowed down. Even
when making only a
slight steering correction,
the bike can be hurled
over the side of the
curve, due to the huge
centrifugal force created
by high-speed riding. The
biker must use both the
front and the rear brakes.
This assures that the
force of deceleration is
divided equally. The
brakes are used to stop,
to reduce speed, and to
maintain control over the
bike.

When braking suddenly, the rider's weight distribution is transferred forward. The front wheel is loaded, the rear wheel is unloaded, and the rider goes over the handlebars. The rider should transfer his weight backwards to offset this weight transfer.

Deceleration is measured in m/sec². The front brake, forcefully applied, can reach approximately 6.5 m/sec², the rear-wheel brake about half that amount. Limited by the law of physics, however, the simultaneous use of both brakes cannot exceed a value of 6.5 m/sec² without flipping the rider over the handlebars, or the bike slipping out from under the biker. This holds true for a normal bike with the biker in a normal position. Increasing the wheelbase and changing the position of the biker (assuming a lower seating position and simultaneously shifting body weight backwards), allows you to brake vigorously without going over the handlebars. This is why a mountain bike designed specifically for downhill riding is lower, and has a longer wheelbase than other mountain bikes. You can make the necessary adjustments in a given situation by lowering the seat and by shifting your weight backwards, as shown here.

On a flat road, the maximum deceleration process for a mountain

bike is sufficient to reduce a speed from 23 mph (10 m/s) to 8 mph (3.5 m/s) in only one second. This is true when either the front brake is used alone or when both brakes are applied. The rear brake alone only slows the bike down to 17 mph (7 m/s) in one second. The rear brake alone isn't enough for controlled and efficient braking.

That the rear brakes are used more often by the uninformed biker is a legacy from the times when bikes were equipped entirely with coaster brakes.

A bike leaning into a curve should not be slowed down by using the front brakes. The bike would lose its ability to adhere to the rising road surface (due to the lateral force of such an action), and the bike might be hurled sideways off the road. It is technically more correct to begin to apply sufficient force to the brakes *before* the curve; braking in the curve would then be unnecessary. If you're already in the curve, and realize that you're going too fast, gently and lightly apply the rear brakes. Sudden, sharp

braking here could result in loss of balance and end in a spill.

What has been discussed until now is relevant only for driving on level terrain. Braking on a steep descent is totally different. In such a situation, typical in open terrain, the biker's weight shifts far forward. The rider would surely pitch over the handlebars if the brakes were applied, even with just moderate pressure. To avoid such a disaster, use *both* brakes, and use them very, very gently. To maintain control of your bike, be sure that you

72

have a good grip on the handlebars. Most of today's modern mountain bikes have "two-finger" brake levers instead of the long brake lever found on older models. These levers are well suited to the situations mentioned previously. Together with today's easy-to-engage brakes, a biker has only to take two fingers of each hand off the handlebars when braking. The one model I recommend, the Magura hydraulic brake, is not yet far enough developed and still comes with a poorly designed brake lever. This brake is extraordinarily efficient. With prolonged braking during steep descent, strong kinetic energy is released. During the braking process, this energy is transformed into heat which must somehow be dissipated. Large metal surfaces, exposed to the air, are ideal for this dissipation. Rim brakes are the most efficient brakes for such situations, because the heat created by the brake pads is absorbed easily. Coaster brakes would overheat. Drum brakes and other, relatively seldom-used brakes (like disc brakes), would function far better,

something that has already been proven: Gary Fisher's mountain bike prototype was equipped with drum brakes. However, drum brakes are considered outmoded.

If you do have a bike with drum brakes, use the front brakes primarily on a lengthy descent that's not too steep. Use the rear brakes, but only sporadically, when maneuvering a curve and when you think you must increase brake pressure. Alternate the use of the front and the rear brakes for other types of brakes. No matter what type you use, avoid using the front brakes when in a curve. Practise the various braking techniques discussed in this chapter somewhere safe before you attempt to tackle narrow trails.

Brake Adjustment

Adjusting caliper brakes is as important and as simple as adjusting the gear-shifting mechanism. Whenever the brake pads wear down, more pressure must be applied for them to work. As the pads wear, the position of the pads relative to the

rim changes. On cantilever brakes they move more to the inside (towards the spokes), while on U-brakes and cam-operated brakes they move in the direction of the tires. To maintain perfect contact with the rim, check and realign brakes once every month. The cable-adjustment mechanism, located at the end of the outer cable of the bowden cable,

Brake-adjustment mechanism

consists of a barrel adjuster and a locknut. Loosen the locknut, screw the barrel adjuster outwards until the tension in the brake cable is effectively adjusted. The brake is properly adjusted when (with the brake lever activated) the distance between the brake lever and the handlebars is about ¾" (2 cm). The final step: Hold the barrel adjuster while tightening the locknut again.

7
Off-Road Riding Techniques

Up into the clouds, and safely down again

Off-road riding differs from riding on normal roads, and the mountain biker must develop suitable off-road riding techniques. These techniques should go beyond those already discussed in chapter 6. The mountain bike gives you a chance to ride your bike away from traffic and congestion and to do so comfortably, quickly and safely. The mountain bike handles differently from ten-speed bikes, because its wheelbase is longer and its frame angles are more relaxed. Your mountain bike's caliper brakes, gears, and its tire tread together all allow you to do things you never thought possible in your wildest dreams.

Tire Pressure

When leaving paved roads and groomed bike paths behind, tire pressure greatly influences the way your mountain bike handles. Just how much tire pressure to use depends upon the surfaces you'll be riding on and, therefore, the pressure must be adjusted accordingly. Take into consideration rolling resistance and shock absorption against the softness of the ground. Minimizing rolling resistance is of primary importance at low speed, because air resistance comes into play only at higher speeds. Rolling resistance is directly related to the "sinkage" of the tire relative to the road surface (see the diagram below). When riding on hard surfaces, sinkage is minimized by increasing the tire pressure to at least 60 psi. On soft surfaces, sinkage is maximized when tire pressure and the give of the surface are equal.

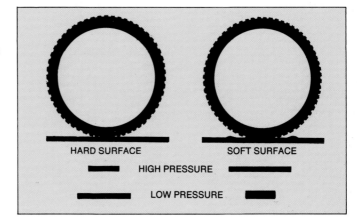

HARD SURFACE   SOFT SURFACE

HIGH PRESSURE

LOW PRESSURE

Therefore, when the surface is soft, the tire pressure must be low (sometimes only 25 psi), while on harder surfaces the tire pressure is correspondingly higher (45 psi). If the surface is uneven, rocky and littered with obstacles, the tire pressure must be high enough to avoid damage to the rim and tires, but low enough so that the rim and tires can act as shock absorbers.

When riding on a severely uneven, rocky surface, lower the tire pressure and reduce riding speed at the same time. The objective in such a situation is to create adhesion. This is achieved by creating as large a contact area of the tire as possible. Use a tire-pressure gauge and try out several different pressures until you have determined which one is the most efficient for the situation at hand.

Mounting and Dismounting Off-Road

When riding off-road, you must be in control of your bike at all times, much more in control than you would be on "normal" streets. In the beginning it might seem cumbersome to learn those necessary skills. If you have children, and if they're familiar with BMX-Sports, take them with you sometimes. Watch them and try to copy the acrobatics they perform.

Mounting the mountain bike off-road can be more difficult than mounting the bike on the road. If you're riding uphill on a steep incline, on loose or soft ground, mounting a bike won't be easy. Proceed as follows:

1. Push the bike from the left side and hold the handlebars with both hands.
2. Select a low gear, but not the very lowest; a 35-inch gear is about the right gear on an uphill. Adjust to a lower gear when riding on flat surfaces.
3. Try to find a 20-foot stretch where the ground surface is reasonably even, even if it isn't a straight path.
4. Position the left pedal about 20° above the horizontal forward position.
5. With a short "running start" (rather than from a dead stop) put your left foot on the left pedal, push the pedal down forcefully while swinging your right leg over the saddle, and then put your right foot on the right pedal.
6. Push the right pedal with your right foot. Make sure that your weight is positioned over the saddle or that your weight is shifted far enough back so that the rear wheel doesn't slide out from under the forward motion. At the same time, don't put too much weight on the front wheel.
7. Engage the appropriate gear and begin to exert enough power (shifting your weight either forward or backwards) to maintain an even, uninterrupted pace. As long as you maintain your momentum, you'll have no difficulty.

Steep Climbs

Often during a climb you'll have to raise yourself up off the saddle and ride standing up. This should be necessary only

Mountain climbing—with a bike and a wonderful view of the Alps

when all available gears have been exhausted, and the climb has to be accomplished through sheer pedal power. This position is used more often just to keep your balance.

Two things can go wrong on loose gravel:

1. The load on the front wheel has been so reduced that steering has become impossible, so the front wheel comes off the ground.
2. The rear wheel loses traction and comes out from under you.

Correct position for hill climbing: standing up

In such situations you must keep a balance between two extremes. This is done when the rider gets out of the saddle and leans forward. The upper body should not lean too far forward over the handlebars; you risk losing steering control, and your rear wheel may lose contact with the ground. A low position will allow you to shift your weight forward or backwards, depending upon the situation. The low position assures good steering control and good surface contact with the rear wheel.

Carrying Your Bike

Sometimes it's necessary to dismount off-road and do some walking over short distances. You'll have to push or carry your bike. You can do this without losing time, and in one smooth motion. Proceed as follows:

1. Decide beforehand where you want to dismount and how you want to proceed from there.
2. Shift into a low gear to prepare the bike for mounting later.
3. Push your body weight forward while standing on the left pedal. Reduce speed necessary for dismounting (at a speed that would allow you to run with your bike without too much effort).
4. Lift your right leg rearwards over the saddle

Sprinting with your bike

78

The moment comes to lift your bike off the ground.

and position it between the bike and your left leg, far in front of you.

5. When you reach the right position, while still running, put down your right foot first. Continue running while you hold the bike at an angle to avoid coming in conflict with the pedal.

6. In very rough terrain, it's often necessary to carry the bike. Hold the handlebars with your left hand while the right hand reaches for the down tube at the bike's center of gravity (about 12″ in front of the bottom bracket).

7. Hoist the (now) well-balanced bike onto your right shoulder, while at the same time reaching with your right hand through the frame for the handlebars. The left hand remains free.

Riding over an obstacle: The arrows show the direction of motion of body and bike in sequence.

Riding over Obstacles

You can overcome some obstacles by riding or rather jumping over them.

A sidewalk curb is an ideal place for practising this maneuver. With the help of your body weight, first lift the front wheel over the curb, and then the rear wheel:

1. Ride towards the obstacle at a moderate speed. Shift your weight forward and off the saddle, standing securely on both pedals. Ride to within 3–6 feet of the obstacle.

2. Pull the handlebars up forcefully while jerking your body weight backwards.

3. As soon as the front wheel clears the obstacle, shift your weight forward until it's on top of the handlebars and the pedals bear no weight. The front wheel will come down while the rear wheel lifts off the ground.

Take time to practise this maneuver. You'll be a master when the front, as well as the rear wheels are actually off the ground at the right moment—not too soon, not too late. Don't jump straight on, but from a slight angle. Usually this technique is used to jump across a ridge or gully in the road surface that runs parallel to your path. The procedure is similar but really much easier because the jump-off point does not have to be gauged so carefully. Drive close up to the obstacle; when you've gathered enough courage, steer briefly away and then head-on towards the obstacle, executing a "forced" curve while simultaneously getting ready to jump.

Crossing Ditches

Riding across a ditch or a gutter is similar to what we've just described. Just reverse the sequence of shifting the body weight. First shift your weight forward, then just before you reach the lowest point, jerk your weight backwards again. The momentum will carry you across the ditch without making you land so hard on the front wheel that the fork is damaged or that the wheel comes to an abrupt halt. If you have enough room on both sides, choose the approach and the drive across the ditch so that your path is as level and as long as possible. During all your maneuvers, keep your eyes on the path that you've chosen.

Off-Road Braking

Downhill riding was what the first mountain bikes did best. However, that made them less agile and less suited for climbing. Maneuverability and climbing ability are emphasized today. Read the remarks in chapter 6 about braking techniques

Shift your weight back when braking on a steep descent

again and reinforce your knowledge of what braking really means, how it works, and how it affects the rider's balance.

Lower the seat when riding downhill and when the ground is uneven. If necessary, the saddle can also be moved backwards. Some seat posts have a second quick-release lever for this purpose. The lowered seat allows the biker to assume the necessary low, stretched-out position. However, don't put your whole weight on the saddle. The saddle should serve as a support, or a

lateral guide for your legs.

Your feet are on the pedals, which are in a "quarter-to-three" (or "quarter-after-nine") position. You're using your legs as "shock absorbers," preventing you from making the most dangerous mistake in this situation—letting your legs dangle. Dangling your legs would cause you to totally lose control over your bike.

This jump was intentional, not accidental. Attempting this maneuver is not recommended.

Drifting

During a steep descent it's often impossible to steer in the manner discussed in chapter 6 (natural vs. forced curves); because high speed and rough soil conditions do not give you enough traction. Under such circumstances use a technique that (sometimes) creates a huge cloud of dust.

Drive up to the turn (barely reducing your speed) and lean with your bike and then yank the front wheel quickly to the inside. The rear wheel will begin to slide to the outside.

This "controlled slide" can be compared to a skier's maneuver. It allows you to change direction when riding at a rather high speed. At the inside of a turn, bring your foot to the ground to brake and to prevent the bike from falling on its side.

Slalom

The technique discussed previously can also be used when going downhill at high speed. As with skiing, this technique requires much body control. Wait until you're sure of how your bike handles during steep descents. Even experienced downhill racers discover that a different bike handles differently from their own.

Causes of Accidents and Injuries

There are several possible causes of mountain bike accidents, including the rider's mistake, another biker's mistake, or the rough terrain itself. The causes can be divided into four groups:

1. Stopping accidents
2. Diverting accidents
3. Skidding accidents
4. Loss-of-control accidents

STOPPING ACCIDENTS

This type of accident occurs when a bike comes to a sudden stop and the biker is either hurled against an obstacle that the bike has collided with, or when the biker falls to the ground.

This can result in serious head injuries or injuries to other sensitive body parts. The risk of having such accidents

Braking hard on a steep downhill slope

can be reduced by adjusting your riding speed to a given situation and by anticipating sudden obstacles. To recognize obstacles early and to have sufficient time to react, don't drive too close to the edge of a trail. Always wear your energy-absorbing helmet.

DIVERTING ACCIDENTS

These spills happen when the front wheel is pushed sideways, usually due to an uneven road surface. The wheels will suddenly go sideways out from under the bike. Here the injuries are contusions, skin abrasions, or fractures (particularly fractures of the hands, shoulders, and sometimes the side of the head). The risk of having these accidents can be reduced by being constantly alert to obstacles in your path. If necessary, maneuver around these obstacles. It is best to cross deep cracks in the ground straight on, and only when the bike does not lean too far to the side. You must be prepared in advance. Make turns that allow you to ride straight over obstacles. When riding

on public roads you must assure yourself that you have enough room for these maneuvers. Look behind you and, if necessary, slow down and wait for the right moment to make your move.

SKIDDING ACCIDENTS

These spills happen when one wheel slides out from under the bike. One of the tires may lose traction due to centrifugal force, or the force of braking may make the wheels go out from under the bike. Injuries here are similar to those described under diverting accidents, but generally they're not quite as severe. Sometimes, when a wheel gives way, it is still possible to avoid an accident. Don't apply the brakes at the very first sign of trouble; steer the bike into the direction of the slide until the bike is again under control.

These accidents are most likely to occur when you ride on smooth surfaces that are covered with either sand, ice, or snow, or even on asphalt covered with wet leaves, or on wet rock, or wet gravel. These accidents can be avoided simply by

avoiding such surfaces under the conditions just mentioned. Look over your shoulder before you turn to make sure that you have enough room and that the trail behind you is clear. When in doubt, wait for the right opportunity. Also, adjust your speed according to the road conditions. Most of all, avoid (at all costs) sudden turns or sudden braking.

LOSS-OF-CONTROL ACCIDENTS

These accidents occur when the biker loses control of his bike. This usually happens when going downhill too fast. The bike leans too far to one side or the other. This lean can't be corrected by steering, and there's not enough room to move on the side to which the bike leans. Sometimes the bike is then carried off the trail, which almost always results in a fall. Here, too, injuries can be rather severe. Avoid these accidents by driving at a reasonable speed. Start applying your brakes early so that you have your bike under control at all times.

8
On the Road and Off-Road

Freedom and independence; touring with your mountain bike

The subject of this chapter is touring, an aspect of biking that is probably of considerable importance to you. Unlike a regular bike, a mountain bike almost begs you to forsake the beaten path and be adventurous. Take a short trip to a nearby place, or a trip to somewhere new, or even go on a tour for several days or weeks. Touring gets you away from the tension and noise of the city streets. The mountain bike is better suited to this task than any other bike. Even if roads are closed or nonexistent (as in the photo on the left, which was taken on a tour through Nepal), the mountain bike will almost always get you to your destination. Whether you ride through familiar territory or if you go abroad, a bike tour is a wonderful experience. The fun is immeasurably increased when the trip is properly prepared. Planning, equipment, packing, and map-reading are all part of the preparation.

Touring with Your Mountain Bike

Some people like to travel alone, while others prefer to tour with a group. Aside from touring with your family or your friends, there are many other possibilities for biking tours. Many group and club tours are offered. Once most of these were budget tours for young people, sponsored by organizations such as American Youth Hostels or bicycle clubs. Today many commercial touring companies offer easy or challenging tours, combining interesting locations and even entertainment. Some trips are expensive, but the price is usually justified by the quality of the program. Touring guides and luggage vans have even taken the last annoying details out of your hands. More and more of these companies now also offer mountain bike tours.

Equipment for a Touring Bike

Perhaps your mountain bike is ready for a tour. This really depends upon the equipment you want to take along and when and where you want to go.

If you'll be driving mostly on asphalt roads, and you plan to stay overnight in a motel or inn, a normal mountain bike without any extras is sufficient. Basically, all you'll need is a credit card and a road map. However, for longer touring (with a tent perhaps), your mountain bike needs to be fitted with special equipment.

We can assume that anybody going on a tour will need and want to take some luggage along. Inclement weather also needs to be taken into consideration. That's why I recommend equipment designed specifically for mountain bikes. Such bikes should have sturdy luggage racks, good lighting systems, proper reflectors, and (perhaps) fenders and water-bottle holders. Find out what kinds of special equipment are available: battery-operated lights, bike computers, and special luggage carriers.

It's easy to attach any one of these items (or exchange and upgrade those that are unsatisfactory) if you don't already have them. A more sturdy carrier, tires with a heavier tread, an improved gearing system (important when touring with luggage), are all easy enough to obtain.

Two bikers and two properly loaded bikes

Luggage

I'm always amazed at how much luggage some bikers can carry on their bikes. Generally they would do just fine with about half of the load. Experience teaches you what's necessary. It's a mistake to take along everything that comes to mind. Overpacking sometimes makes you forget the really important items. Think about what's really needed—planning really pays off.

After each trip, unpack as carefully as you packed before the trip. Separate your belongings into four categories:

1. Those items you need that can't be replaced
2. Things you didn't use this time but will need on the next trip
3. Things that you used but that could be replaced by other items from the first category, or of which you won't need as many
4. Those items you didn't use, and which you

Possible arrangement of panniers on a bike. The most practical arrangement is the example in the middle.

know you can do without.

In this way you reduce the weight of your luggage, because you will find that you can exchange heavy items for similar lightweight items, and that you can do well without certain items.

PACKING

Think when you pack your panniers. Things that belong together should be packed together—you won't have to rummage through everything to look for a particular item. Whatever is needed for a picnic ought to be in one pannier. Rain gear and road maps ought to be easily accessible. Valuables ought to be kept together and should be in a bag which can be easily removed from the bike. Over time, and with a little bit of thought, you'll have a system that works best for you.

How can you attach the luggage to your bike? Practical experiments have shown that the method depicted on the middle bike in the illustration above provides the greatest stability, the most efficient weight distribution, and is the one that interferes the least with your control of the bike.

Divide your luggage so that part of it is loaded low in front. Whatever goes in the back does not necessarily have to be as low, as long as it is positioned as far forward as possible. The panniers have to be positioned in such a way that they do not interfere with the bike's operation. Make sure that the panniers are securely fastened, on top and below. Test by turning your bike upside-down. Properly secured

luggage won't come loose. Hold the bike by the handlebars and shake it vigorously from side to side. If the bike does not sway back and forth, the luggage is secured well.

The true test, however, comes when riding the bike. If nothing interferes with pedalling, then everything is okay. At the beginning of the trip, you won't mind that your heel has to move slightly out of the way to avoid hitting the back pannier with every crank revolution. By the end of a long day in the saddle, you'll change your mind. Take a test ride at the beginning of your tour and change the arrangement until you can move without hindrance. Just getting used to riding with a loaded bike is a chore, so make sure that you can actually pedal comfortably.

A peaceful setting for an overnight stay

Overnight Camping and Provisions

Although the last section emphasized luggage, it was not meant to suggest that bike touring necessarily includes camping out overnight in a tent and eating simple campfire meals. Going on a bike tour does not necessarily mean giving up comfort. Wanting a comfortable bed, a hot shower, and a sophisticated atmosphere after a hard day's ride is as justified as it is after a day's car trip. On a bike trip, you might as well pay for comfort with the money you've saved on transportation.

Getting There and Getting Back

A bike tour can't always begin and end at your own front door. If you have planned on touring distant places, how will you reach the starting point? Take public transportation! If you go on a two- or three-week tour, don't park your car for that long a time in a strange place. Only luck will get you a secure parking place! Leave your car at home and take public transportation. Get the necessary information for shipping your bike, including the cost. Sometimes you can take your bike along with you, at other times you must send it ahead. In general, a big city is not a convenient place to start a biking tour. Dealing with urban traffic, just getting out of a strange city is often so complicated that it's not worth the trouble. Consider, therefore, starting in a smaller town.

90

Flying represents a whole new set of problems. Some travel agents give information that turns out to be false when you arrive at the airport. Most of the time, your bike will go on the same flight with you. Most airlines in the United States will charge you a hefty fee for doing so. In addition, some airlines insist that the bike be packed in cartons or carrying cases. The latter are rather expensive, but your bike will be well protected. A carton that fits your bike can be bought from a bike dealer. If you can't find a storage place for the carton, you'll need a new carton for the return trip. That should still be simpler than finding a storage place for the carton, or easier than finding and paying dearly for a carrying case.

Maps and Orientation Aids

Part of bike touring is planning your trip and being able to find your way. This is not as easy off-road as it is on well-marked roads. The landmarks you've chosen for orientation might not be marked on *any* map and you would be *totally* lost.

Plan your trip in stages. Start with a map with a scale of perhaps 1:300,000 that will give you a sense of the area. It allows you to interpret factors such as elevation, rivers, population density, etc. From this information determine if the region you're interested in is really suitable for a bike tour at all.

Then get a normal road map with detailed information of a general area. From that map you can find out how to reach the area you have chosen, how to find the main roads, and how dense the traffic might be. Use this road map to plan your tour roughly without deciding on specific details.

Now it's time to consult a topographical map, such as the USGS "quad" series. Maps made specifically for bikers often emphasize certain trails at the expense of other important details. The mountain biker needs a detailed map on a scale of at least 1:25,000, and no more than 1:100,000. For day trips only use maps with 1:25,000 or 1:50,000 scales.For longer trips, use a scale of 1:100,000.

When touring, always keep your map handy. Don't wait until you're lost before you use your map. The best map won't help you find your way back if you can't determine where you are at the moment and at what point you got lost. Reading a map takes practice, and you can only practise when you use your map frequently. This holds true when you plan your trip, and when you're actually on your way. Map-reading is an important skill, if you're in a strange country or just on a one-day trip close to home.

9
Fitness and Biking

No pain, no gain: mountain biking is for the physically fit

Using the mountain bike will almost certainly add to your general fitness. Training for the sport is a strenuous activity in itself. As you train for the sport, your overall stamina and conditioning will improve. The long-term benefits of biking are well known.

Fitness Training with Your Mountain Bike

The mountain bike is an ideal exercise machine. What makes this (and any other bike) different from other exercise equipment is its overall practicality. Your bike allows you to combine physical exercise with practical goals—it gets you where you want to go.

The belief that biking is healthier than other endurance sports (like running or rowing) is false. With an equal amount of energy expended, a bike only increases your speed, it doesn't increase the efficiency of your training. What you can't do when rowing, or when running, is to leave your front door and take care of a couple of errands while still exercising.

If you engage in sports on a regular basis, you'll get more out of life; you'll be healthier if you stay fit. Endurance training (on a bike or elsewhere) makes energy available to the body under aerobic conditions.

The body has several ways of converting food into energy. The maximum output that can be maintained for a longer period is called the anaerobic threshold. If the physical activity remains below this limit, the energy made available is controlled with the help of the oxygen available in the blood. The maximum aerobic activity level depends on the cardio-pulmonary system, specifically the heart. The blood absorbs and gives off oxygen as it flows through the veins and arteries to the muscles. "$\dot{V}O_2$-max" is the value which indicates how much oxygen can be used over time. It is possible to sustain an activity over a long period of time under aerobic conditions, because the body uses oxygen at the same rate as it's taken in, and because no lactic acid is produced in the muscle

$$\text{Thr} = 60 + \text{Ti}\,(\text{Mhr}^* - \text{Rhr})$$
$$^*\text{Mhr} = 220 - \text{age}$$
Ti (training intensity)
varies from .6 (low)
to .85 (high)

The training heart rate (Thr) equals 60 plus the product of training intensity (Ti) times the maximum heart rate less the resting heart rate (Mhr—Rhr). The maximum heart rate is calculated at 220 beats per minute, less the individual's age. Training intensity can range from 60–85% of the individual's maximum heart rate. The resting heart rate can range from 60–80 beats per minute.

This formula should be familiar to anyone who's ever taken a good aerobics class. The object of a good workout is to maintain a training heart rate over a period of time, usually 20 minutes per session.

Let's try out the formula for a thirty-year old:

First, calculate the maximum heart rate: $220 - 30 = 190$

Now, plug that figure into the formula.
$\text{Thr} = 60 + .7\,(190 - 60)$

Observed trials are an exciting form of competition, in which dexterity, rather than speed, is of the essence.

tissue. Lactic acid is generated during anaerobic activity, causing heaviness in the muscles. For reasonably fit people, the aerobic metabolism is sufficient to sustain a performance of 200–300 watt. It is possible to increase this level of performance with training.

There is an easy way to check the level of your performance, which is based on the connection between $\dot{V}O_2$ and heartbeats per minute or pulse rate. Measuring heartbeats per minute will give us this information. The training heart rate can be calculated as follows:

94

Thus, a 30-year-old person must maintain a pulse rate of 151 beats/minute for training to be effective. Training must take place at least three times a week and last for at least 20 minutes each time. Most people underestimate the effort involved, because they believe an activity to be quite intense when, in reality, it is considerably below the training limit and, consequently, it doesn't result in an increase in performance. It is best to check your pulse regularly, while training and under normal conditions. Take your pulse in the morning (just after arising) for 15 seconds, multiply that number by 4 to calculate your resting pulse rate. As long as your resting pulse rate decreases (or if it doesn't increase or fluctuate), assume that your fitness program is working.

A Training Program

Try to find a route that you can ride without having to stop. Begin your training with a moderate warm-up and end it with a cool-down period. Choose a stretch of road or trail where you can ride for 30 minutes. Ideal conditions are not easy to find everywhere.

The stretch of road you choose should be relatively flat at the beginning. It should then become more difficult, and then for the cool-down, it should become easy again.

1. Start with a middle gear on a flat road, riding slowly; Increase your speed until, after 5 minutes, you have reached your training heart rate.
2. Maintain this speed for 20 minutes, and check your pulse occasionally.
3. After 20 minutes, slow down gradually, until after 5 minutes your pulse is about 20–30 beats below your training heart rate.
4. If you train more than four times a week, the amount of time spent with the heart at the training heart rate can be reduced to 10 minutes per session.
5. Move about for 10 minutes, and wait before jumping into the shower. You'll feel more refreshed.

Other Exercises

If you truly want to be in control of your bike, do other exercises as well, and on a regular basis. Included are stretching, breathing exercises, and weight lifting to increase strength. Gymnastics and stretching exercises are particularly effective for relaxed and comfortable biking. Limber muscles greatly influence your performance level. Warm up with some light running before starting your exercises, particularly during cold weather.

Strengthening exercises are usually done using exercise machines or free weights. Don't concentrate only on the muscles that you use for biking. Rather, train the muscles in your arms, stomach, back, and neck.

Finally, some general tips on health. Extreme exertion, insufficient liquid intake, or overexposure to the sun are potentially as dangerous as some crashes or traffic accidents.

10
Care and Maintenance

Treat your mountain bike well, and it will treat you well

A mountain bike is asked to perform under the most difficult conditions, and you don't want it to let you down. Although it's ruggedly constructed, a mountain bike still needs care and maintenance. The bike must be cleaned and checked regularly and any mechanical defects must be fixed. In addition, a mountain biker must be able to take care of any problem while on the road. It is beyond the scope of this book to discuss every repair and maintenance job in detail. Some necessary repairs are better left to the experts. However, with the help of a good repair manual you can learn how to do much of what is necessary. Repair manuals with more specific instructions are easily available.

Tools

Depending on the difficulty of the terrain and the length of your trip, it will be necessary to carry some tools in your luggage. The following are suggested for normal conditions:

- Small adjustable wrench
- Small screwdriver
- Compressed air refill
- Tire-repair kit
- Spoke wrench
- Tire irons
- Allen wrenches
- Chain tool
- 13- and 14-mm open-end/box wrenches

Long trips in unfamiliar territory require you to be prepared for many different situations. Take time to find out which tools and which spare parts are necessary to have with you, and in what sizes. Assemble the necessary tools and spread them out in front of you. To pack them, roll them up in a rag or make a pouch with individual compartments for each of the tools. The pouches for the tools should be far enough apart so that the cloth can be easily rolled up. Leave a few pockets empty for eventual additions to your collection. Find a place on the bike for the pump and the larger spare parts. The spokes, for instance, could be attached to one of the frame tubes or perhaps you might be able to squeeze spare spokes inside the pump or inside the handlebars.

A wet bike needs special care.

Preventive Maintenance

Major repairs can often be avoided by inspecting your bike on a regular basis and by performing simple maintenance. Establish a plan for your weekly, monthly, and twice-yearly maintenance. The maintenance does not have to be time-consuming. If a quick check will tell you what you have to do, do it. Eventually you'll save yourself much trouble. This chapter describes how to schedule your bike's care.

Weekly Inspection

HANDBRAKES

- Hold the bike by the handlebars, using both hands. Apply the front-brake lever while trying to push the bike forward at the same time. With the brake engaged, there should be ¾" (2 cm) space remaining between the brake lever and the handlebars.
- Test the rear brake in the same way. With

your hand on the saddle, push the bike forward.

- If necessary, make adjustments according to the information given under "Brake Adjustment" on page 118.

TIRE PRESSURE

- Both tires should be adequately inflated and the valves should be securely in place.
- If necessary, add air or do the required repair. Make sure you always have your pump and a repair kit with you.

WHEELS

- Lift the front wheel off the ground, spin it slowly and see if it rotates freely and comes to rest with the valve at the bottom. Do the same with the rear wheel.
- Hold the bike firmly either at the front fork or at the seat stays, and then rock the wheel rim from side to side to see if the hubs are tight.
- If necessary, let a repair shop adjust the hub mechanism.

HANDLEBARS AND SADDLE

- The handlebars and the seat should be at their proper heights, and tightened securely.
- Make any adjustments necessary.

GEARS

- Check that the gear shifters are in their proper positions, tightened securely, and that they operate easily.
- Lift the rear wheel off the ground and check to see if you can engage every gear—move the shift lever and turn the crank arm to do this.
- If necessary, make the proper adjustments.

VISUAL INSPECTION

- Look over your bike and see if everything is as it should be. Check for any loose or missing parts.
- Tighten, adjust, or replace whatever is necessary.

Monthly Inspection

In addition to the weekly routine, do a thorough monthly checkup. Do the necessary repairs and adjustments. Pay particular attention to the following:

CLEANING

Specific instructions for cleaning your bike (you might have to clean it more than once a month) are given later in this chapter.

GENERAL CHECKUP

Check carefully to see if all the parts, nuts and bolts are properly secured. Tighten what is necessary and replace missing or damaged parts.

BALL BEARINGS

Check to see if the ball bearings of all movable parts (hubs, bottom bracket, pedals, steering) move freely without play, resistance, or noise. If necessary, adjust, lubricate, or overhaul the bearings.

BRAKE CABLES AND GEAR CABLES

Check to see if the bowden cables for the brakes and the gears move freely and if they're properly adjusted. If necessary, correct, lubricate, or replace the cable(s).

TIRES

Hang the bike on a hook or turn it upside-down and carefully check to see if both tires are in perfect condition. Remove any debris embedded in the tread. If necessary, repair or replace the inner tube and/or outer tire.

WHEELS

Spin the wheels to see if they move smoothly and if the rim seems to wobble sideways. The rim should be adjusted if the wheel wobbles.

WHEEL ALIGNMENT

Check to see if the rear wheel "tracks" with the front wheel (i.e., whether the two wheels are in perfect alignment). If not, the fork or frame might be bent or one of the wheels might not be centered properly. Ask a repair shop to double-check the alignment and repair what's necessary.

BRAKES

Check to see if the brake pads project at least ³⁄₁₆″ (5 mm) beyond the brake blocks, and if the surface of the block is completely in contact with the rim. If necessary, correct as described in "Brake Adjustment" on page 118.

CHAIN

If the chain is dirty, or if it squeaks, remove, clean, and lubricate it.

GEARS

Before making any adjustments, clean and lubricate all parts of the gear mechanism with a light oil. Remove the excess oil when you're finished.

LUBRICATION

Follow the instructions found under "Lubrication" on this page.

SIX-MONTH INSPECTION

If you use your bike all year, I recommend that you inspect it both in the fall and in the spring. If you use your bike only during better weather, inspect it at the end of the season. At the beginning of the next season only a monthly inspection will be necessary.

The six-month inspection includes *all* the jobs that were previously discussed under "weekly" and "monthly" inspection. In addition, do the following:

- Remove, clean, lubricate, and reinstall (or replace) the chain.
- Remove, check, lubricate, and reinstall (or replace) the brake cables and the gear cables.
- Adjust and lubricate every ball bearing, or have them replaced.
- Sand all rust spots and repaint where necessary.

- Protect exposed metal parts with wax, vaseline, or chrome polish.
- Replace any part that's missing, damaged or functioning improperly.

Cleaning

Here are detailed suggestions for cleaning your bike properly and in a systematic way, something that might seem simple, yet is seldom done properly:

1. Loosen and remove dust and dirt with a rag or a brush.
2. Wipe off any remaining dirt with a damp cloth. If necessary, use lots of water, and a sponge or a rag, and dry off the bike thoroughly afterwards. Prevent water from penetrating the ball bearings of the wheels, the bottom bracket, the pedals, or the headset.
3. Greasy dirt can be removed using a solution of kerosene or turpentine to which 5% mineral oil is added. Prevent the cleaning solution from penetrating the ball bearings; this might dissolve necessary lubrication.

4. Cover the end of a screwdriver with a rag and remove hidden dirt from nooks and crannies (around the chain rings, the sprockets, the derailleurs, and the brakes).
5. Protect all exposed metal parts by applying a thin film of petroleum jelly or wax with a clean rag. Afterwards, using a dry cloth, remove any excess protectants from the places where you hold your bike, or where the bike comes in contact with clothing.
6. Turn the bike upside-down and look for any dirt you might have missed.

Lubrication

The diagram on page 104 shows all the points where a bike should be lubricated regularly. Remove all dust and dirt before lubricating. Here's a list of those parts that need lubrication and suggestions about how to lubricate them.

CHAIN

At least once a month, treat the chain with a

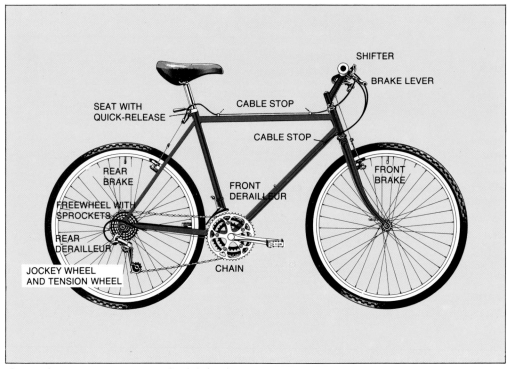

Parts of the bike needing regular lubrication

special chain lubricant, available in spray cans. First, however, clean the chain. Remove any excess lubricant when you're finished.

BRAKE CABLES AND GEAR CABLES

Once a month lubricate the portion of the gear cable where it enters the casing. Remove any excess lubricant. If the cable has to be removed or replaced, coat the inner cable with petroleum jelly before inserting it back into the casing.

GEARS

Once a month, after a thorough cleaning, lubricate the gears with spray-can oil. Direct your attention to all moving parts and adjustment mechanisms, the derailleur, as well as the chain rings. Remove any excess lubricant.

Usually, indexed gearing systems only need cleaning, they don't have to be lubricated. Replace the bowden cables (cable and casing) at least once a year, making sure that you don't pinch the casing and that the ends of the inner cables are not frayed.

BALL BEARINGS

Once a year remove, clean, lubricate with ball-bearing grease, and reinstall all ball bearings. This might be one job that you'd like to turn over to a bike-repair shop.

BRAKES

Monthly, after careful cleaning, lightly lubricate all the moving parts on the levers, the brake arms, as well as on the controls. Remove any excess lubricant. Make sure that the brake blocks and the wheel rims have not come in contact with the lubricant.

Important Maintenance

Here are instructions for maintenance and repair work. They are grouped together according to their function: steering, wheels, drivetrain, gears, and brakes.

Adjusting the Handlebars

The height of the handlebars is adjustable on every model. The angle of the extension is adjustable only on those models where the extension is separate from the handlebars. The handlebar-height adjustment on mountain bikes is usually

a bit cumbersome because the brake cable interferes when the handlebars are pulled upwards. If your bike is like this, the cable has to be removed first and readjusted after the proper height has been established. For further information, see chapter 3 on saddle and handlebar positions.

Mounting and Removing the Wheels

This procedure is necessary when making repairs and also when the bike has to be packed for shipping. Depending on the hub type, proceed as

follows when removing or mounting the wheels:

WHEEL WITH AXLE NUTS

Tools and equipment
- Wrench
- For the rear wheel: rags and a screwdriver

Removal
1. Loosen both axle nuts with 4 rotations. Turn the axle nuts on the front wheel just as far as necessary to loosen them, along with the front-wheel retaining devices.
2. At the rear wheel, pull the chain back, and then move the wheel forward until the chain can be removed.

Direction for routing the chain

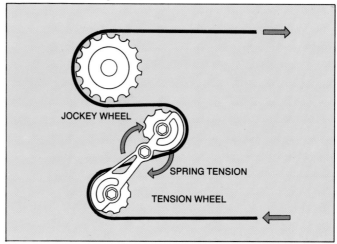

105

3. Remove the wheel. If the rim brake gets in the way, loosen the connecting cable of the cantilever brake or U-brake on one side.

Installation

1. Guide the nuts, the washers, and the wheel retaining devices towards the end of the axle without removing them.

2. Engage the gear so that the chain lies on the smallest chain ring and on the next-to-smallest sprocket.

3. Guide the axle into the drop-out of the frame or the fork. For the rear wheel, engage the chain in the smallest or the next-to-smallest sprocket, while the rear derailleur is held back and the chain is guided around the mechanism.

4. Tighten the axle nuts while holding the wheel in its proper position. Tighten the brake cables and the gear cables and adjust everything properly.

WHEEL WITH A QUICK-RELEASE HUB

This type of hub is now used for most high-quality mountain bikes and

Removing a wheel with a quick-release hub is easy.

hybrids. The locknut is strictly an adjustment device and may not be used to loosen or tighten the wheel. After the locknut has been properly adjusted, the wheel is installed or removed by flipping the quick-release lever.

Tools and Equipment
● For the rear wheel: rags

Removal

1. Preparation is the same as for a wheel with axle nuts.

2. Move the quick-release lever to the "open" position. If the wheel is

not loose enough, turn the locknut 1 or 2 times by hand.

3. Proceed in the same manner as for a wheel with axle nuts.

Installation

1. Preparation is the same as for a wheel with axle nuts.

2. Move the quick-release lever to the "open" position. If necessary, loosen or tighten the locknut (with the lever in the "open" position).

3. Continue as for a wheel with axle nuts.

Fixing a Flat

Although the tires on a mountain bike are particularly rugged, a flat tire is still the biker's most frequent problem. Here's how to repair or replace the inner tube and the tire. If you have to repair a tire, follow only those instructions that are relevant for your task. In all cases, put rim tape between the rim and the inner tube. This tape prevents the tube from being damaged by the spoke ends.

Tools and equipment

- 3 tire irons
- Tire-repair kit
- Pump

Sequence

1. First check the valve; sometimes air escapes from here. If necessary, tighten the valve cap or replace the inner portion of the valve (possibly replacing only the rubber portion of a Dunlop valve). If that doesn't solve the problem, read on.
2. Check the tire inside and out and remove any embedded objects—nails, thorns, or glass fragments; note the spots where you found these objects.

Lift the tire off the rim using tire irons at 6″ (15 cm) intervals.

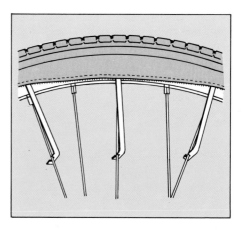

3. Let the remaining air escape by opening the valve (press down on the pin on Presta and Schrader valves). Remove the nut.
4. Push the valve housing inside the rim and push the tire towards the middle of the rim, all the way around.
5. Hook the long end of the tire iron (positioned directly opposite the valve) under the tire, lift the tire off the rim while hooking the other end of the tire iron to a spoke.
6. Hook the second tire iron 6″ (15 cm) further down, under the tire and proceed as above (see the diagram above). The first tire iron can now be removed and the tire can be lifted over the edge of the rim.

7. If necessary, repeat the procedure, using the first tire iron that was just removed, until the whole tire can be removed from the rim.
8. Pull the inner tube out at the valve.
9. Inflate the inner tube.
10. Find and mark the spot from where the air is escaping from the inner tube and mark that spot. If you can't easily find the spot, and you can't hear the air escaping, rotate the tube past your eye, or submerge the tube section by section in water. Mark the spot(s) where you see air bubbles escape.
11. Dry the inner tube, sand the damaged area, and wipe it dry, covering an area somewhat bigger than

the size of the patch.

12. Apply rubber patch solution to the tube evenly and let it dry for approximately three minutes.

13. Remove the backing foil from the patch and securely press the adhesive side down on the prepared area; the transparent foil on the patch remains in place.

14. Inflate the inner tube as much as necessary to see that no air is escaping. If necessary, remove the patch and repeat the procedure.

15. Check the interior of the tire and the inside of the rim. Remove any debris or anything that could possibly damage the inner tube. File down any spoke ends that protrude from the rim. Cover the inside of the rim with rim tape.

16. Deflate the inner tube.

17. Guide the valve from the inside through the valve hole in the rim and fasten the valve nut.

18. Very lightly inflate the inner tube and place it on the rim, under the tire.

The tire must be inserted evenly into the rim.

This is how to push the remaining portion of the tire back over the edge of the rim.

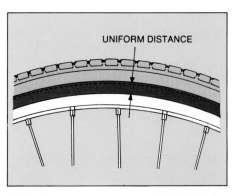

UNIFORM DISTANCE

19. Push the tire over the edge of the rim by hand, pushing it into the middle of the rim. Start this procedure about one foot (30 cm) away from the valve, working in the direction opposite to it until you reach a point on the other end one foot in front of the valve.

20. Deflate the inner tube, force the tire into the deep section of the rim and, working from both sides of the valve at the same time, pull this portion also (by hand) over the inside edge of the rim.

21. Push the valve into the rim once again to make sure that this portion is also properly seated.

22. Lightly inflate the inner tube and push

the tire back and forth to make sure that no portion of the inner tube is caught under the edge of the tire and that the cover is concentric with the rim. The distance between the edge of the rim and the sidewall marker must be the same all the way around the tire. See page 108.

23. Inflate the inner tube.
24. Make the necessary adjustments and tighten all the parts that have been loosened.

Replacing the Spokes

Spokes may break under conditions such as high-speed riding on rough terrain. Since every spoke is an integral part of the whole wheel, a broken spoke should be replaced as soon as possible. It pays to have replacement spokes (of the same length and thickness) and nipples on hand. See the drawing below.

Most of the time you can install a new spoke with an old nipple. If the nipple is damaged, or the spoke and the nipples can't be turned because of rust accumulation, you must remove the tire, the inner tube, and the rim lining so that the nipple can be replaced.

The most vulnerable spokes are those that carry the heaviest load—the spokes on the rear wheel on the side of the chain ring. In order to replace those spokes, you

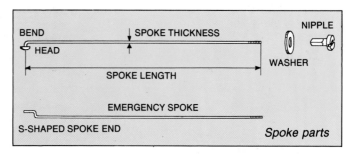

Spoke parts

Increasing spoke tension using the spoke wrench

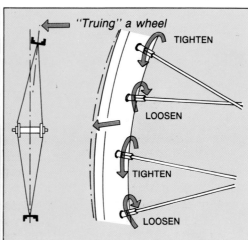

must remove the free-wheel sprockets. You can spare yourself this job on the road if you carry oversized spokes without a head bent to make emergency spokes. See the drawing below.

Tools and Equipment
● Spoke wrench
● Lubricant

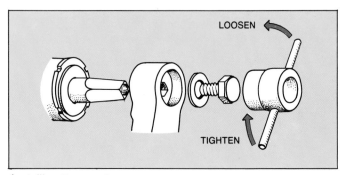
Installing the crank

Procedure
1. Remove or replace a damaged spoke by unscrewing the nipples.
2. Observe the spoke pattern which is repeated after every fourth spoke. Check the position of the head of the spoke (it's either on the inside or the outside), the direction of the spoke, and how it crosses the other spokes.

Tightening or loosening the crank using a crank-removal tool and a wrench.

3. Lightly lubricate the end of the thread and position the spoke matching the existing pattern. Screw the spoke into place.
4. Tighten the nipple until the tension is equal to those spokes already mounted.
5. Check to see if and where the wheel is out of "true" by spinning the wheel *very* slowly and observing the distance between the brake block and the side of the rim. Mark the out-of-true places.
6. Where the rim is pulled to the right, loosen the spokes that lead to the right hub flange by ½ to 1 turn and tighten those that lead to the opposite direction. See page 110.
7. Increase the tension in all the spokes. Insufficient spoke tension is often the cause of

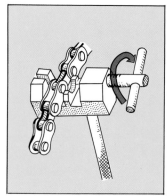
A chain held in place in the groove, allowing the pin to be removed.

spoke breakage and wheel problems.

Procedure
Remove the dust cap. Tighten the nut or the bolt using the crank wrench. See page 110. Replace the dust cap.

Chain Maintenance or Replacement

The chain should lie in the smallest chain ring

and in the second-smallest sprocket.

Tools and Equipment
- Special chain tool
- Cleaning solution (either turpentine or kerosene to which 5% mineral oil is added)
- Brush
- Rags
- Chain lubricant

Chain removal
1. Insert the chain tool into a pin far enough for the tool to touch the pin.
2. Hold the chain and the tool in place and turn the lever about 6 times. Be sure that the pin is not totally pushed out.
3. Remove the chain tool.
4. Separate the chain with a slight twist, and then remove the chain.

Maintenance
Submerge the chain in a mixture of turpentine or kerosene and 5% mineral oil; remove any dirt with a brush and allow the chain to dry; lubricate the chain with a special chain lubricant.

Installation
1. The chain length is correct when it has a little spring to it after being installed over the largest chain ring and

the largest sprocket, and guided through the front derailleur, and the rear derailleur, as shown on page 105. Remove or add links as needed.
2. Connect the chain by carefully pushing the pin through the links until it extends equally on both sides.
3. Loosen the chain links by gently twisting the chain back and forth.
4. If the chain "jumps" or slides off the smallest sprockets (something that happens when a new chain is mounted with old sprockets), the sprocket must also be replaced.

Adjusting the Derailleur

Sometimes it is impossible to adjust indexed gears to correct shifting problems or chain-jumping. For the latter problem, check first to see if either the derailleur itself or the drop-out is damaged. If either is damaged, let your repair shop do the work. If not, do the following:

If, when shifting, the chain moves beyond the largest or the smallest sprocket, or beyond a chain ring, the respective

(front or rear) derailleur must be adjusted. This work is best done with the bike suspended from the ceiling or turned upside-down.

Tools and Equipment
- Small screwdriver
- Rags (in case the chain has jumped off completely)

Procedure
1. If necessary, put the chain back in place and bring the gear shifter into the position that causes the problem.
2. Determine the nature of the problem. Did the chain move too far (or not far enough) to the inside (left), or to the outside (right)? Is the front or the rear derailleur affected?
3. Each derailleur has two adjustment screws (in different places on different models). These screws have a spring underneath the screw head to prevent unintentional movement of the screw due to motion vibration when riding. One of the screws limits the side movement of the derailleur to the inside (left), and the other limits the movement to the outside (right).

4. If the screws are not marked with an H (adjustment of the highest gear) and an L (for the lowest gear), you must determine which screw does what. To find out, move the gear shifter, watch the direction of the movement of the derailleur, and see which screw affects that movement.
5. Tighten the one screw to limit the movement of the derailleur (in case the chain went too far) or loosen the other screw to allow for more movement (if the chain did not reach far enough).
6. Check every gear combination, preferably while the bike is suspended upside down.

● Continue until all the gears engage properly.
● If the cable is too loose or too tight, make the necessary adjustments. See the material following.

If the adjustments did not achieve the desired result, check the following:

1. Inner cable: if it's damaged, replace it.
2. Outer cable cover: if it's bent, replace it.

3. Cable stops and the derailleur mounts on the frame, and the shifter must be securely attached. Tighten them if necessary.
4. Mounting clamp of shifter: must be tight enough for the shifter to stay securely in place.
5. Crank arm and chainring mountings: both can develop play; adjust/tighten, if necessary.

● SunTour and Campagnolo mountain bike gear systems have an additional screw which limits the angle of movement of the derailleur's attachment bolt. One or two turns in the proper direction are often helpful to either loosen or tighten the screw.

Adjusting the Derailleur Cable

Have all necessary adjustments completed (see the previous instructions), and then choose the gear that positions the chain on the smallest sprocket and on the smallest chain ring.

Tools and Equipment
● Wrench

Procedure
1. Hold the adjusting barrel and loosen the clamp nut; tighten or loosen the adjusting barrel; hold the barrel again and tighten the clamp nut.
2. If the front derailleur does not have an adjusting barrel, or if there is not enough room for adjustments, loosen the clamp nut by one or two turns. Pull out the cable or relieve the cable tension; tighten the clamp nut.
3. Check all the gears and, if necessary, continue adjustment.

Maintenance of Derailleurs and Indexed-Gearing Systems

TOOLS AND EQUIPMENT

● Small screwdriver
● Pliers and cone wrench, if needed
● Appropriate Allen wrench, if needed

Procedure
1. If possible, position the shifter in the "F"-position (for "friction," or non-indexed shifting),

113

and engage the highest gear: the largest chain ring with the smallest sprocket.

2. Tighten the rear derailleur cable until it is taut, but not under tension. Adjust the adjustment barrel or the clamp nut to do this.

3. Now engage the lowest gear (the smallest chain ring, with the largest sprocket) again, with the lever in the F-position.

4. Engage the highest gear, and choose the "Index" setting.

5. Engage the next-to-lowest gear with the shifter. If the derailleur does not move the chain to the next-to-smallest sprocket, the adjustment barrel must be tightened by one half-turn. If the derailleur goes beyond the next-to-lowest gear, the adjustment barrel must be loosened. Continue adjusting the barrel until the gear engages properly and smoothly.

6. Continue tightening the cable at the adjusting barrel or the clamp nut until you can hear a sound that tells you that the chain is making contact with the third-smallest sprocket (with the chain on the second-smallest sprocket). Now turn the adjustment barrel, but only until the sound stops.

7. Test all the gear combinations to assure yourself that they can all be engaged without difficulty. If necessary, make further adjustments.

Note

If you haven't been able to properly adjust the shifters according to the instructions given, you might have to replace the shifter.

Brake Adjustment

A properly functioning rear brake will stop the rear wheel completely when the bike is pushed and the brake lever is activated and if the wheel rim and the brake blocks are dry. The same holds true for the front brake. Applying the front brake will cause the bike to tilt forward. If brakes lose their power, start to drag, squeak, or "wobble," clean the rim first. If that doesn't solve the problem, the brakes must be adjusted. Should that also prove ineffective, the

brakes must be over-
hauled or replaced.

Tools and equipment
● Wrench and pliers

Procedure
1. Hold the barrel adjus-
   ter, and loosen the
   locknut.
2. To loosen the brakes,
   turn the barrel adjuster
   in; to fasten again, turn
   it out.
3. Hold the adjuster bar-
   rel and tighten the cable in its new position
   with the clamp nut.
4. If this procedure does
   not solve the problem,
   turn the adjuster barrel
   all the way in (loosening the brakes). Where
   applicable, loosen the
   quick-release. Loosen
   the brake-cable clamp,
   pull or loosen the
   brake cable, and
   tighten the mechanism
   in the new adjusted
   position.
5. Test and continue ad-
   justing, if needed.

Note
Most mountain bike
brake levers have an ad-
justment screw with
which the distance be-
tween the handlebars
and the levers in passive
position can be adjusted.
Adjust the screw so that

the lever can be comfort-
ably reached and the dis-
tance between the levers
and the handlebars in an
active position is at least
¾″ (2 cm).

Replacing the Brake Cable

You might want to re-
place a brake cable when
you perform your 6-
month maintenance
schedule. This will save
time, eventually, and it
will make your bike more
dependable. Carry a
spare brake cable when
on a long tour. Keep in
mind that there are bow-
den cables with different
nipple ends, depending
on the make of bike for
which they're designed.

Tools and equipment
● Wrench
● Needle-nose pliers
● Wire cutters (or special
  cable-cutting pliers)
● Lubricant

Removal
1. Remove one end of
   the connecting cable
   from the brake while
   squeezing the brake
   arms together.

2. Loosen the brake-ca-
   ble clamp nut and ca-
   ble carrier and pull out
   the cable. Don't lose
   the cable carrier and
   the connecting cable!
3. Activate and release
   the brake lever a few
   times to loosen the cable. Push the cable
   and the nipple deeper
   into the brake lever until the nipple can be
   disengaged.
4. Pull the brake from the
   nipple, catching the
   spring.

Positioning the brake blocks

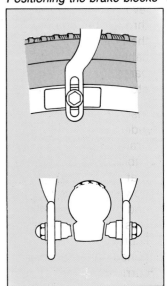

Installation

1. Check if the inner and outer cable are okay (i.e., long enough, free of rust, neither knicked nor frayed).

2. Determine the length of the outer cable (or its parts): as short as possible but without the possibility of bending when turning the handlebars.

3. Cut the outer cable without creating a "hook" on the end. Remove about ¼″ (6 mm) of the plastic covering from both ends and attach the ferrule (if applicable).

4. Lubricate the cable, beginning at the brake lever. Guide the cable through the channel of the brake lever, outer cable, adjusting the barrel and the cable stops on the frame.

5. Insert the nipple in the indentation in the brake lever; pull the cable taut and tighten it at the opposite end; now clamp the free end of the cable. Cables on cantilever and U-brakes are positioned over the cable carrier and hooked into the brake arms.

117

6. Adjust the brake-cable tension and all necessary parts. Close the brake pads.

Replacing Brake Blocks

This is necessary whenever the rubber of the blocks is worn down or worn unevenly. Replace the complete block (block and brake shoe).

Tools and equipment
- Wrench (for some models, an Allen wrench)

Procedure
1. Relax the brakes by taking out the nipple at the connecting cable on one side.
2. Remove the nut or bolt and washer of the brake shoe.
3. Remove the brake shoe.
4. Repeat steps 2 and 3 on the other side.
5. Tighten the brakes and adjust them.

Brake Adjustment

Brake blocks that don't touch both sides of the rim equally can usually be corrected by straightening the wheel. The wheel may be poorly centered in the frame.

The problem can also be the result of a twisted rim or a misaligned wheel. If this isn't the case, the brake itself must be adjusted. In most cases the adjustment screw at one of the brake arms can be either turned inwards or outwards until the distance between the brake shoe and the rim is equal on both sides of the wheel. Regular cantilever brakes are adjusted by bending the spring (using two pairs of pliers) in the appropriate direction until the brake shoes are positioned equally on both sides of the rim.

Development Table (in Metres) for 26″ Wheels

Number of teeth on chain ring

	24	26	28	30	32	34	36	38	39	40	41	42	43	44	45	46	47	48	49	50	51	52	53	
13	3.80	4.10	4.50	4.80	5.10	5.40	5.70	6.10	6.20	6.40	6.50	6.70	6.90	7.00	7.20	7.30	7.50	7.70	7.80	8.00	8.10	8.30	8.50	13
14	3.60	3.90	4.10	4.40	4.70	5.00	5.30	5.60	5.80	5.90	6.10	6.20	6.40	6.50	6.70	6.80	7.00	7.10	7.30	7.40	7.60	7.70	7.90	14
15	3.30	3.60	3.90	4.10	4.40	4.70	5.00	5.30	5.40	5.50	5.70	5.80	5.90	6.10	6.20	6.40	6.50	6.60	6.80	6.90	7.10	7.20	7.30	15
16	3.10	3.40	3.60	3.90	4.10	4.40	4.70	4.90	5.10	5.20	5.30	5.40	5.60	5.70	5.80	6.00	6.10	6.20	6.40	6.50	6.60	6.70	6.90	16
17	2.90	3.20	3.40	3.70	3.90	4.10	4.40	4.60	4.80	4.90	5.00	5.10	5.20	5.40	5.50	5.60	5.70	5.90	6.00	6.10	6.20	6.30	6.50	17
18	2.80	3.00	3.20	3.50	3.70	3.90	4.10	4.40	4.50	4.60	4.70	4.80	5.00	5.10	5.20	5.30	5.40	5.50	5.60	5.80	5.90	6.00	6.10	18
19	2.60	2.80	3.10	3.30	3.50	3.70	3.90	4.10	4.30	4.40	4.50	4.60	4.70	4.80	4.90	5.00	5.10	5.20	5.40	5.50	5.60	5.70	5.80	19
20	2.50	2.70	2.90	3.10	3.30	3.50	3.70	3.90	4.00	4.10	4.30	4.40	4.50	4.70	4.80	4.90	4.90	5.00	5.10	5.20	5.30	5.40	5.50	20
21	2.40	2.60	2.80	3.00	3.20	3.40	3.60	3.80	3.90	4.00	4.10	4.20	4.20	4.30	4.40	4.50	4.60	4.70	4.80	4.90	5.00	5.10	5.15	21
22	2.30	2.50	2.60	2.80	3.00	3.20	3.40	3.60	3.70	3.80	3.90	4.00	4.10	4.15	4.20	4.30	4.40	4.50	4.60	4.70	4.80	4.90	4.95	22
23	2.20	2.30	2.50	2.70	2.90	3.10	3.20	3.40	3.50	3.60	3.70	3.80	3.90	4.00	4.10	4.15	4.20	4.30	4.40	4.50	4.60	4.70	4.80	23
24	2.10	2.20	2.40	2.60	2.80	2.90	3.10	3.30	3.40	3.50	3.50	3.60	3.70	3.80	3.90	4.00	4.10	4.15	4.20	4.30	4.40	4.50	4.60	23
25	2.00	2.20	2.30	2.50	2.70	2.80	3.00	3.20	3.25	3.30	3.40	3.50	3.60	3.70	3.70	3.80	3.90	4.00	4.10	4.15	4.20	4.30	4.40	25
26	1.90	2.10	2.20	2.40	2.60	2.70	2.90	3.00	3.10	3.20	3.30	3.40	3.40	3.50	3.60	3.70	3.80	3.85	3.90	4.00	4.10	4.15	4.20	26
27	1.85	2.00	2.20	2.30	2.50	2.60	2.80	2.90	3.00	3.10	3.20	3.25	3.30	3.40	3.50	3.55	3.60	3.70	3.80	3.80	3.90	4.00	4.10	27
28	1.80	1.90	2.10	2.20	2.40	2.50	2.70	2.80	2.90	3.00	3.05	3.10	3.20	3.30	3.35	3.40	3.50	3.60	3.65	3.70	3.80	3.90	3.90	28
30	1.70	1.80	1.90	2.10	2.20	2.40	2.50	2.60	2.70	2.80	2.90	2.95	3.00	3.05	3.10	3.20	3.30	3.35	3.40	3.50	3.55	3.60	3.70	30
32	1.60	1.70	1.80	1.90	2.10	2.20	2.30	2.50	2.55	2.60	2.70	2.75	2.80	2.90	2.95	3.00	3.05	3.10	3.20	3.25	3.30	3.40	3.45	32
34	1.50	1.60	1.70	1.80	2.00	2.10	2.20	2.30	2.40	2.45	2.50	2.60	2.60	2.70	2.75	2.80	2.90	2.95	3.00	3.10	3.15	3.20	3.25	34
38	1.40	1.50	1.60	1.70	1.80	2.00	2.10	2.20	2.25	2.30	2.40	2.45	2.50	2.55	2.60	2.70	2.75	2.80	2.85	2.90	2.95	3.00	3.10	38
	24	26	28	30	32	34	36	38	39	40	41	42	43	44	45	46	47	48	49	50	51	52	53	

Number of teeth on sprocket

Gear Table for 26″ Wheels

Number of teeth on chain ring

Number of teeth on sprocket

Sprocket	24	26	28	30	32	34	36	38	39	40	41	42	43	44	45	46	47	48	49	50	51	52	53	Sprocket
13	48	52	56	60	64	68	72	76	78	80	82	84	86	88	90	92	94	96	98	100	102	104	106	**13**
14	45	48	52	56	60	63	67	70	72	74	76	78	80	82	84	85	87	89	91	93	95	97	98	**14**
15	42	45	49	52	55	59	62	66	68	69	71	73	75	76	78	80	81	83	85	87	88	90	92	**15**
16	39	42	45	49	52	55	58	61	63	65	67	68	70	72	73	75	76	78	80	81	83	85	86	**16**
17	37	40	43	46	49	52	55	58	60	61	63	64	66	67	69	70	72	73	75	76	78	80	81	**17**
18	35	38	40	43	46	49	52	55	56	58	59	61	62	64	65	66	68	69	71	72	74	75	77	**18**
19	33	36	38	41	44	47	49	52	53	55	56	57	59	60	62	63	64	66	67	68	70	71	73	**18**
20	31	34	36	39	42	44	47	49	51	52	53	55	56	57	59	60	61	62	64	65	66	68	69	**20**
21	30	32	35	37	40	42	45	47	48	50	51	52	53	54	56	57	58	59	61	62	63	64	66	**21**
22	28	31	33	35	38	40	43	45	46	47	48	50	51	52	53	54	56	57	58	59	60	61	63	**22**
23	27	29	32	34	36	38	41	43	44	45	46	47	49	50	51	52	53	54	55	57	58	59	60	**23**
24	26	28	30	32	35	37	39	41	42	43	44	45	47	48	49	50	51	52	53	54	55	56	57	**24**
25	25	27	29	31	33	35	37	39	41	42	43	44	45	46	47	48	49	50	51	52	53	54	55	**25**
26	24	26	28	30	32	34	36	38	39	40	41	42	43	44	45	46	47	48	49	50	51	52	53	**26**
27	23	25	27	29	31	33	35	37	38	39	39	40	41	42	43	44	45	46	47	48	49	50	51	**27**
28	22	24	26	28	30	32	33	35	36	37	38	39	40	41	42	43	44	45	46	46	47	48	49	**28**
30	21	23	24	26	28	29	31	33	34	35	36	36	37	38	39	40	41	42	42	43	44	45	46	**30**
32	20	21	23	24	26	28	29	31	32	33	33	34	35	36	37	37	38	39	40	41	41	42	43	**32**
34	18	20	21	23	24	26	28	29	30	31	31	32	33	34	34	35	36	37	37	38	39	40	41	**34**
38	16	18	19	21	22	23	25	26	27	27	28	29	29	30	31	31	32	32	33	34	35	36	36	**38**
	24	**26**	**28**	**30**	**32**	**34**	**36**	**38**	**39**	**40**	**41**	**42**	**43**	**44**	**45**	**46**	**47**	**48**	**49**	**50**	**51**	**52**	**53**	

Frame-Size Chart

Inseam length	Recommended frame size		Straddle height
	A	B	C
in	in	in	in
29	14	13	25
30	15	14	26
31	16	15	27
32	17	16	28
33	18	17	29
34	19	18	30
35	20	19	31
36	21	20	32
37	22	21	33
38	23	22	34

Note: All these values are approximate

Note: Recommended seat-tube length: The maximum size is approximately 1″ (2.5 cm) longer; the minimum size is 1″ (2.5 cm) shorter.

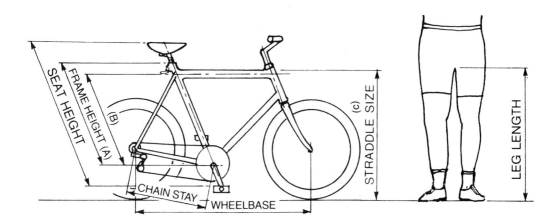

Troubleshooting Guide

Problem	Possible cause	Solution
bike hard to ride (high resistance when coasting and pedalling)	1. insufficient tire pressure, incipient flat tire	inflate and/or mend tire
	2. tire or wheel rubs on brake, fork, chain stay, or fender	adjust and center brake; adjust or straighten wheel; install narrower tire if insufficient clearance
	3. poorly moving drivetrain	lubricate, adjust or clean drivetrain
bike hard to pedal	1. dirty chain, chain ring, freewheel sprocket or gears	clean and lubricate
	2. insufficient lubrication on chain or derailleur	lubricate, clean
	3. bottom bracket or crank arms not sufficiently lubricated, or damaged	remove, clean, lubricate, adjust or replace, overhaul
chain jumps off chain ring or sprockets	1. derailleur out of adjustment	adjust derailleurs or gears
gears do not engage properly, chain slips or jumps	1. shift lever dirty, loose or damaged	clean, adjust, lubricate or replace
	2. derailleur cable anchor or guides loose, or cable dirty or corroded	tighten attachments and cable screws or replace cable
	3. derailleur or gears out of adjustment	adjust derailleur or gears
	4. chain too short or too long	correct or replace

Problem	Possible cause	Solution
	5. new chain on old chain rings/sprockets	check chain, replace sprockets
	6. chain links bind or chain not sufficiently lubricated	twist chain sideways, clean and lubricate chain
inadequate braking	1. rim or brake blocks wet, greasy or dirty	clean rim and brake blocks
	2. brakes incorrectly adjusted	adjust brakes
	3. brake cable doesn't move freely	replace damaged cable
	4. bowden cable installed wrong	correct installation
	5. bowden cable moves poorly	remove, clean, lubricate
	6. brake blocks worn	replace
	7. wrong brake pads	get right pads
brakes squeak	1. brake shoes loose	adjust brakes and tighten shoes
	2. brake blocks worn	replace
	3. rim or brake blocks dirty	clean rim and replace blocks
	4. cheap brakes	replace with better
irregular pedalling movement	1. crank arm or pedal loose	tighten cranks and pedals
	2. pedal, crank arm, bottom bracket bearing out of adjustment	adjust or overhaul, tighten or replace
	3. crank arm, chain ring or pedal axle bent	replace or get straightened (by experts)

Metric Equivalents

Inches to Millimetres and Centimetres
MM—millimetres   *CM—centimetres*

Inches	MM	CM	Inches	CM	Inches	CM
1/8	3	0.3	9	22.9	30	76.2
1/4	6	0.6	10	25.1	31	78.7
3/8	10	1.0	11	27.9	32	81.3
1/2	13	1.3	12	30.5	33	83.8
5/8	16	1.6	13	33.0	34	86.4
3/4	19	1.9	14	35.6	35	88.9
7/8	22	2.2	15	38.1	36	91.4
1	25	2.5	16	40.6	37	94.0
1 1/4	32	3.2	17	43.2	38	96.5
1 1/2	38	3.8	18	45.7	39	99.1
1 3/4	44	4.4	19	48.3	40	101.6
2	51	5.1	20	50.8	41	104.1
2 1/2	64	6.4	21	53.3	42	106.7
2	76	7.6	22	55.9	43	109.2
3 1/2	89	8.9	23	58.4	44	111.8
4	102	10.2	24	61.0	45	114.3
4 1/2	114	11.4	25	63.5	46	116.8
5	127	12.7	26	66.0	47	119.4
6	152	15.2	27	68.6	48	121.9
7	178	17.8	28	71.1	49	124.5
8	203	20.3	29	73.7	50	127.0

INDEX

Photo Credits

Bainbridge, Gordon: 33, 54, 56, 74, 79, 83, 94, 100/101, 102
Birkner, D.: 97
Campagnolo: 20, 61
Glogowski, Dieter: 81, 86, 90, 98
Hochschorner GmbH: 52
Kahlich, Eddy: 48, 49, 50
Kuwahara: 19, 23, 25, 34, 45, 60, 73
Muddy Fox: 39
Renner–Centurion: 2, 6, 20, 26, 28, 29, 40, 55, 64, 68, 72, 77
Schlüter, Andreas: 27, 35, 53, 67, 70, 78, 82, 84, 96
Smolik, Hans-Christian: 8, 38, 43, 44, 61, 62, 106, 108, 109, 110
Specialized: 12, 21
Trek: page 61
van der Plas, Neil: 88
Witek, Peter: 44/45, 50, 63, 92, 112, 115, 117

About the Author

Robert van der Plas is a recognized expert on biking and bike technology. His books and articles dealing with the different aspects of biking have been published here and abroad. He is also familiar with the practical side of biking. He uses the mountain bike to run his daily errands as well as riding it for pleasure.

Since the early 1980s, he has watched with interest the development and use of the mountain bike. His first book on mountain biking was published in English in 1984. In this book he discusses, from firsthand experience, how to best handle the modern mountain bike.